I Sought and I Found

Other books by the same author,
published by Orbis Books

Blessed Are You Who Believed
I, Francis
The God Who Comes
Letters from the Desert
Love Is for Living
Summoned by Love

I Sought
and I Found

My Experience of God and of the Church

CARLO CARRETTO

Translated by ROBERT BARR

ORBIS BOOKS
Maryknoll, New York 10545

Second Printing, February 1985

First published as *Ho cercato e ho trovato,* second edition revised and enlarged, copyright © 1983 by Cittadella Editrice, Assisi.

English translation copyright © 1984 by Orbis Books, Maryknoll, NY 10545

Typeset in Great Britain and printed and bound in the United States of America

Orbis ISBN: 0-88344-203-5 (cloth)
          0-88344-202-7 (paper)

Contents

Acknowledgement

The majority of Scripture quotations are taken from The Jerusalem Bible, copyright © 1966, 1967 and 1968 by Darton, Longman and Todd Ltd, and Doubleday and Company Inc. and are used by permission of the publishers.

Introduction: I Sought and . . . I Found

A few years ago, a book by Augusto Guerriero (Ricciardetto) appeared with the title *Quaesivi et Non Inveni*: which being translated into ordinary language means 'I Sought and Did Not Find'.

I may say that it was not the book itself that got me excited. It was really a rather disconnected, superficial book. But its title was a real bombshell: 'I Sought and Did Not Find'.

Now, how could such a thing possibly have happened? After all, the object of the 'seeking' was obviously God himself.

I sought God and did not find him!

Could this really have happened?

It certainly looked absurd to me. It not only contradicted a saying of Jesus in which I believe most profoundly, 'Seek and you shall find', but I also had to ask myself: What sort of a God is this, then, who does not allow himself to be found?

What is he playing, hide-and-seek?

Does God actually hide from someone who goes honestly looking for him?

This sort of God simply has no right to exist. This would be the negation of his essence, which is Life, Light, Love.

And besides . . . he is called the Creator, the Immense, the Marvellous One.

And as if that were not enough, the Wonderful. And as the Muslim rosary, the *subha*, has been praying for centuries, he is the King, he is Beauty, he is the Mighty, he is the Great, the Glorified, the Magnificent, he is Providence, he is the Majestic One, the Wise, the Splendid, the Unconquerable, the Holy One, the All-Knowing, the Present. He is Newness, he is the Unchangeable, the First, the Last, the Manifest, the Witness, the Mighty, the Good, the Glorious, the Sublime.

No, it cannot have happened.

It is impossible to stand and look up at the sun and say 'The sun does not exist'.

Or to press a button on an electronic brain and decide that the answer is ridiculous.

Or to send a magnetic impulse up to a satellite, and have the satellite suddenly answer you with a photograph or other piece of scientific data you have been seeking, and then just to say 'Hmmm . . . what a coincidence'.

No, it cannot have happened.

And so I felt like writing to Ricciardetto, and saying 'Dear Brother: I saw your book title. Do you know what I thought? I thought you went to the ocean, took off all your clothes, walked across the beach, put your toe in the water, walked into the water until it was up to your ankles, then your legs, then your chest, then your neck. Then you started swimming. You even tried swimming under water. You came back out on the beach, put your clothes back on . . . and you said to some people there: "Water? What water?"

'I once heard a Jewish proverb that goes like this: "The last thing a fish sees is the water." Now, really! Nor can the birds see the air they live in. But try depriving them of it . . . then see how they flounder.

'Don't you know, brother, that we are like fish and birds for much of our lives and only become aware of water and air, once we are deprived of them?

'Perhaps this is God's somewhat drastic way of revealing himself; out of consideration for our immaturity, he reveals himself in negative. We are not ready to see his positive. That takes time.

'The truth is, we do not perceive his presence when all is going well, but we shudder when he is not there or falls silent.

'What you assert makes me feel like smiling, even though you have used catch-phrases that I have heard thousands and thousands of times before. Be that as it may, I remain unconvinced.

'I do not question the truth of what you say, nor your

claims about having sought but not having found. What I do question is your use of terms.

'Just what do you mean by "God" when you tell me you haven't found him?

'I have a strong suspicion that we are talking at cross-purposes here, and that the colossal density of contemporary atheism, so blithely broadcast by huge masses of people, is more a question of language than of reality. It is as if we were back in Babel. We no longer possess the same language.

'You say you don't see God. And I see you immersed in him like a fish in water. I *see* this.

'We are no longer using the same name for the same thing.'
Let me explain.

Beyond question, we live in an era of transition – transition of a vastness and scope never seen before.

What has occurred in this century, and is still occurring, is of proportions no other era has ever witnessed.

We have come of age, we are told. We have arrived at human adulthood. The past, for the sons and daughters of today, is really 'passed'.

Everything has grown old. The new generations seem to be starting all over again at the beginning. Nothing escapes ruthless criticism and review. And not always in a humble, friendly spirit, either.

When I go to a friend's house and find his son, for instance, in front of the television, I have a strange sensation of distance – and an even stronger one of alienation, of being estranged – from the boy.

And it is not my fault.

If I say hello, often the youngster does not answer me, and his weary eye regards me as if nothing of interest could come of my being around.

It can happen too – and it is by no means a rare occurrence – that an ill-concealed scowl will steal across the youngster's face. Or even worse, armed with an invisible, diabolical rocket, he gestures as if to get rid of me, just as if he were the interplanetary giant who fills his fantasy and heart.

Péguy used to say that today's generation gap was unbridgeable. He was a prophet.

Behold the electronic age. Behold a time of technology refined to improbable degrees of sophistication. Behold a time of crashing idols, and even more, of falling ideologies of the past. A time too of desecration.

Even the Church, the mightiest and most steadfast pillar of all, faced with history's change of course and the statistical evidence for this, contemplates the changing times and gasps for breath.

Those really abreast of what is going on feel like ships in a storm. They are beginning to think about having to jettison certain items, accumulated over the course of the centuries, and of sticking strictly to essentials until the storm is weathered.

If I were to say how I see human beings today, I would have to tell you that I see them naked, and I mean really naked. Terribly mature and adult, but really naked.

And as the one who is naked looks for something to wear in order to survive, human beings today, not finding anything in which to clothe themselves, cast about for just anything at all, even clothing torn to tatters by the tempest.

As a result the naked one is poorly clad in clothes that stink of age and are totally out of date.

I have said that it is a question of language. Now I shall say that it is a question of clothing. Or, better, of language and of clothing: that is, of culture.

Many people, when they state 'I do not believe in God', do not know precisely what they are trying to say. Many people, when they think of God, find themselves standing before him in a garment long since out of fashion, and absolutely incompatible with their modern mentality.

In my youth, before the Council [the Second Vatican Council], I read the Bible imagining, with scrupulous certitude, that the tree of Eden was really a tree, that the apple was really an apple, that Adam had his birth certificate in his pocket with his name on it, and that his wife, Mrs Eve, was right there at his side, looking at him dutifully and respectfully. If I read the Bible that way today I would simply not be able to accept it.

How far the Spirit has brought us, even in this storm! And what a wonderful new garment he is preparing to cover our nakedness!

Many, having preferred to stay in rags, sniffing the odour of must, can no longer stick the out-of-date cut of their religious culture, as archaic as an out-of-date nun's habit.

In a nutshell . . . reading Ricciardetto's book, and listening to people tell me 'I sought and did not find' – one thing leaps out at me and hits me: they are all of them galloping full tilt against their past.

They have grown up – but the loincloth that once covered their 'sex', and upon which they had written 'God', is strange and unfamiliar now, and they no longer understand it – like the fig leaf of Eden.

They think it was really a fig leaf! And all the while it was really only an image, a sign, useful for explaining certain mysterious things.

In my long experience with young people, I have discovered that their crises of faith appear in two stages.

In the first stage they construct an idea, a concept, of God, absorbing all manner of images and sketches of him from past culture as if they were actual things. In the second stage they erase these images in a rage, all these pictures and sketches they have made for themselves – because their mentality, which has become scientific and mature, finds them outmoded and unacceptable.

I went through the same thing.

How I flailed out against my past!

How many shots I fired against the distorted idea of God I had made for myself!

I only stopped shooting when no image remained.

Now I no longer shoot because I no longer know where to shoot.

Today I no longer see the phantasm of God that I had built for myself. I seek only to feel his presence.

And this is enough.

And I feel it everywhere, enveloped though it be in immense, sublime, raw mystery.

I feel it in the never-failing tokens God sends me, the signs that declare his Reality to me, like water, sun, night, or fire.

I feel it in history.

I feel it in silence.

I relish it in hope.

I seize it in love.

Now that I have understood, I refuse to allow myself any sketch, any image, any daydream, in thinking of God, and I content myself with thinking of him as the Real One surrounding me, in which I am immersed.

And the Real One is there indeed – gazing on me in his Might, in his Beauty, in his Logic, in his Transparency – and he forces himself upon me in three words I cannot erase, even with all this devilish rationality of mine: Life, Light, Love.

You see, these three words – and this is the marvel of marvels – are actually three Persons too:

The Person of the Father, who is Life.

The Person of the Son, who is Light.

The Person of the Holy Spirit, who is Love.

Yes, God is a Person for me. Nor am I surprised.

Am I not a person too?

This is why the catechism tells me that I am created in his image and likeness: precisely because I am a person, and cannot deny my selfhood any more than I can deny the reality of my body and my spirit, in which I live and by which I am manifested.

Yes, God is a Person for me, and I communicate with him.

I listen to him.

I speak to him.

He gives me peace, and the joy of living.

He awakens me each morning with his word (cf. Isaiah 50:4).

He is so near me!

He comforts me.

He chides me.

He is my soul and heart's repose.

He is my all.

I have no wish to offend the memory of Ricciardetto in writing this book.

I liked him, and I always admired him in his search for God, though I did think he engaged in it in rather too cultural a way, and a tiny bit pretentiously.

Now he is in the Light.

Word of his death reached me in Japan one sunny Sunday while I was visiting the temple of Kamakura, some hundred kilometres from Tokyo.

It was a marvellous morning. And for the Japanese it was the day the birth of life is celebrated.

Prospective bridegrooms were escorting their brides-to-be before the great Buddha – gathering with them on the steps of the temple, and presenting them to him. The young women were arrayed in their finest kimonos. Young mothers, too, were carrying their newborn babies there, to have them prayed for.

I was enchanted by all this beauty, and by such throngs of people at prayer!

And if Ricciardetto had been there with me, he too would have been moved, to behold such vitality, such hope.

Look how many are 'finding'! I would have told him.

How many have found!

See how they love one another!

See how they hope!

Don't be afraid!

God is the Living One.

Yes, Ricciardetto gave me the title for this book. But the idea had been inside me for a long while. I might say it was born of my actual experience of God as I walked hand in hand with him down the pathways of my life.

I have had the good fortune to live on the cusp of two eras – two times, a before and an after.

I am old enough to have known the time we today call the 'past': the time of immobility, of tradition, the time of the 'little old world', when a boy and girl still treated each other formally on first being introduced, and got to know each other only gradually – a time when engaged couples preserved their virginity until marriage, and preserved it out of conviction. And then I have lived in the modern scramble, too, enough not to be scandalized when I see a high percentage of couples going off and living together today without so much as dreaming of getting married – not even before the registrar.

I have known the Africa of my father, and then the Africa of the Democratic and People's Republics.

I have known the way of the camel, and then I have seen the great oil refineries transform the desert into a Babel of money and ugliness.

I was there to hear the traditional moralists, before the Council – Lefebvrians, we would call them today – state that you could commit mortal sins by the hundreds, by omitting the fixed rubrics of the Latin liturgy. And I have had occasion to see Mass celebrated without vestments, without a chalice, with a red scarf worn round the priest's neck.

Yes, I have seen a thing or two!

I have seen the transition, the 'passage'.

I have seen the times a-changing!

New times are here!

But I have also seen the Council!

For me, that immense concourse of bishops gathered around Pope John and Pope Paul was the grandest proof of the presence of the Spirit in the Catholic Church today.

No other Church has been able to do as much!

It was like going back to the first Council, in Jerusalem, with John, James, Peter and Andrew.

What a cornerstone to build tomorrow on – the milestone to start out from to walk down the roadways of today's world.

Yes, we might as well come right out and say it. There is a radical change going on. And there is a still more radical stability.

The change is in culture, and in custom. The stability is in the faith.

The change is in the world, which has turned pagan again. The stability is in the Church, which is still ready to repeat the message of salvation.

It is as if we were back at the beginning.

We are like the first Christians.
We are back in the times of the little Gospel communities.
We are in apostolic times.

When an era begins – when a human being begins over again
– the primacy should be given to faith.

Culture – even culture steeped in faith – comes later.

Men and women do not follow Christ in culture, they follow
him in faith.

When Paul faced the scholars of Athens and decided to
play the scholar himself, he fell flat on his face. He did not
try the experiment again. From then on, he was content to
speak of nothing but Jesus Christ and him crucified (cf. 1
Corinthians 2:2).

Strange . . . but this is the way it is: between faith and
culture there is a continuous process of getting married and
getting divorced.

And humanity's weakness on earth is its inability to lock
up the invisible in visible dimensions, and furnish a container
for what the whole world cannot contain.

In the effort – which is inevitable, owing to our need for
knowledge – history is made, and the everlasting spiritual
exodus is cloaked in the continual contradictions of our
earthly exoduses. The face of God is sketched in the horrid
distortions of our sick hearts, and Light is cloaked in the
shadows of non-light.

Inevitably the story of humanity is a great, continuous
distortion of the Truth, the story of the dismaying limitations
of our capacity to love.

This is the agony of generations on the road, the sign of
their radical poverty to live the Divine, the everlasting exodus
of man.

Perhaps it was because I straddled two eras, or perhaps it
was because I thirsted for the Absolute – all the more surely
because I was being called by him – but I felt the urge to
run away.

I had no wish to start building the houses of my culture
all over again right on the spot where the earthquake had

razed them. I had no wish to repair my spiritual unity by staying where I was, as most people asked me to do.

The stones of the old city no longer fitted together properly.

I wanted to get away. I felt a thirst for silence and prayer.

It was naked faith that attracted me. This alone seemed the anchor of salvation for my weary spirit.

Any cultural cloak for the Word seemed a distortion.

Any attempt at compromise seemed an enfeeblement of my urge to follow Christ Crucified.

Any rite, especially a flashy one, seemed to be mere rhetoric, while human beings were suffering.

The desert – the real desert, the one made out of jackal howls and starry nights – was the place of my encounter with God.

No longer did I seek miraculous or mythical signs of his activity. I sought the nakedness of his presence.

No longer did I wish to discuss him. I wanted to know him.

No longer did I seek the rapport with him I had so often enjoyed in the Sunday liturgy – which can so easily give you the illusion of being 'right where it's at', with its rites and ceremonies. Now I desired his intimacy in the nakedness of matter, in the transparency of light, in the toil of loving my fellow human beings.

I sought the God of all seven days of the week, not the God of Sunday.

It was not hard for me to find him! No!

It was not hard because he was there ready waiting for me. And I found him.

And this is why I say with joy, and dare to testify to my brothers and sisters in the Spirit: *I sought and I found.*

CARLO CARRETTO

Part One

EXPERIENCE OF GOD

1 First Experience of Life

I was born in Alessandria by ... well, you might say, by accident.

The city had no connection with my family. We had our true stock, our deep roots, in the Langhe hills, where my father and mother were farmers, with all the sweetness, strength and piety of that marvellous country in their blood.

But Alessandria became my parents' temporary moorings. Young marrieds then, they had left their home to find employment. They had left behind them the rural civilization in which, God be thanked, they had rejoiced for generations and generations – and which they still carried with them, along with the few household goods to which they had fallen heir from their parents, who had remained up there in the old hamlet, to fade sweetly away like the light of an autumn sunset.

I should like to say something about this young family's displacement. It is something that comes to my mind whenever I think of the numberless such migrations occasioned by unemployment, need, or at times by unforeseen cataclysms like floods or earthquakes.

My father told me the story. He told me how devastating the year had been for the countryside – how hail had fallen with unheard-of violence for that part of the country, destroying everything. The worst was that the disaster had not come in August, when hail was fairly usual in the Langhe region, and would batter only the vineyards then. But it had come in June, when not only are the vines vulnerable, but the harvest is standing in the fields.

In short, that year the hail had destroyed absolutely everything: grain and grape, maize and greens.

Nothing was left.

My father told me how the young people of the countryside, in the face of this disaster, had met together and decided to go down to the plains in search of work. They knew that the harvest there required a great many hands, and that they would quickly find work.

He told me – I can still hear his voice – 'We left in the evening, and walked all night – the whole sixty kilometres – down to the plain, where farms were big and work was plenty.'

The vision of that platoon of youth has remained stamped in my mind – young people refusing to yield to adversity, striding in hope towards a toilsome, tough tomorrow.

I remember, as if it were today, the expression on my father's face; and he added: 'Just think, Carlo – after hiking all the night long, we started reaping in the fields next morning as if we had been peacefully in our beds all night.'

That is the way to go, boys and girls!

I remember I looked at my father with admiration. I felt him close to me – and great, precisely in the function of a father, who, by telling the story of his own hard past, had imparted to me something very important: a sense of courage and hope.

My father had not asked himself whether God could exist if he was able to ignore human suffering, or was so distracted and insensitive as to permit cataclysms and hailstorms to pound down on the heads of the poor.

No, he had not wondered about that. For him, and for my mother, the God that existed was the God of hope – the God who made you get on your feet again, out of the rubble of the earthquake, the God who pushed you, impoverished by the scourge of the hail, to begin over again without any fuss, and force yourself to find inside yourself the strength to start out down the road again – and not look to others for everything as if they owed it to you – but above all to free yourself from the bitterness that seeing injustice can give you, or from the surprise of not being helped.

The God of my father was the God of life, the presence always present, always alive and operating within one.

He was the God who does not give you permission to fling yourself on the ground in despair and say 'It is all over!'

It is not true that it is all over. It all changes. And you had better be ready, willing and able when the change comes, even if it presents itself to you as something hard – and especially if it presents itself to you as something incomprehensible. Who knows? Perhaps this change, this novelty, can bring you something good!

After all . . .

After all, the new, the unforeseeable, has always been the product of disaster.

And this was certainly no small factor in my family's story.

You see, my father ended his story by explaining that this misfortune had so shaken him that he took it into his head to leave his native countryside and go looking for work somewhere else.

He spoke to my mother and she agreed.

He took an examination, and qualified for a job with the State Railways. That was how we landed in Alessandria, where I was born, and where two years later my brother was born. But then we headed for Turin, in search of more suitable surroundings for poor people to rear their adolescent children in. We set up house in an outlying, lively district of the city, where there was a little bit of everything, but especially a little bit of everything we needed.

The hail had been a misfortune. That was a fact. But it was also a fact that the hail was why we landed in this quarter, where we were lucky in making many young friends and where – and this was the height of good luck for us – there was a little oratory of Don Bosco.

How much that oratory meant to us!

How much it meant to my mother to have that little church on Via Piazza, where she went to pray and gather strength!

Herein is contained the mystery of the history of our salvation – the mystery of our continual exoduses, of this constant getting up and moving out, invited and impelled by a force which, when we do not recognize it, we call fate, but which, when we are clear about it, and aware, we call the will of God.

Do you believe that everything is part of a plan, a design, an intervention of God in our affairs? I do. And I am convinced that God's love can transform the darkness of a disaster or the irrationality of an earthquake into an event that can influence, or even completely change, our lives.

Ours was certainly changed. And for the better.

Finding ourselves, in adolescence, in a place so conducive to the development of our faith, and so rich in wonderful encounters, furnished our migrant family with an effective aid to becoming more socially adult, more open to good.

It was in this very place that my brother's missionary vocation sprang up, and later the religious orientation of my sisters, leading both of them to veil and vows.

Years later, when I was studying philosophy, I came upon this passage in Augustine: 'God can permit evil only in so far as he is capable of transforming it into a good.' And in the light of my own experience, I turned my father's story over in my mind.

And then Augustine's saying seemed to me all the truer.

My family was Christian. That was a fact. I was born to the faith in this family. I learned to pray at my mother's knee, to fear God, to go to church, not to blaspheme, to join in the processions, and to put up the crib when Christmas drew near.

When I think of my childhood piety, traditional, rather static, and somewhat lacking in creative thrust – I still cannot help but find extremely worthwhile values.

Even today I am struck by the unity that faith and culture, the human and the divine, prayer and peace, Church and family, imagination and reality, God and man, produced in me.

I had not as yet read the Book of Genesis, where it tells how God placed man in the Garden of Eden, to till it and guard it. Yet I felt myself to be in a garden, within the confines of my own world, of my vocation, and was aware of a relationship with Him who strolled beneath the trees of the garden, gradually revealing his invisible presence to me.

I did not as yet know Jeremiah, who tells the story of the potter fashioning his clay, who tirelessly refashions the pot that breaks in his hands, shaping another vessel from the same clay (Jeremiah 18:1–6). But I did feel myself to be in the hands of a God who continuously refashions us and never tires of changing the plans he has made for us when we resist him with the poverty and fragility of our clay.

Yes, my family helped me lay the foundations of faith and hope. And I feel such gratitude for that Langhe region, where I sucked up life, and where the people of the soil kept the calendar of the saints within easy reach, staking out the seasons with the great religious feasts, knowing how to cast their seed into the furrows while invoking St Lucy and St Roch, firm in the certainty of a bond between heaven and earth, between rain and prayer, between the happiness of board and bed and the divine order of things.

We shall never be able to say enough about the importance of a popular piety rooted in the flesh and blood of the poor, and slowly ripened over generations, even though – as is only natural – slightly muddled or tinged with a pinch of superstition, yet ever dominated by and enveloped in an immense, unique and solemn mystery: God.

What strength!

What poetry!

What a wellspring of courage and true heroism!

Today, precisely because so many lack it, spoiled by wealth and too comfortable a life, we can appreciate the danger and gravity of its lack.

All these insecure, disorientated young people!

What sorrow there is in houses void of the divine, impoverished by lack of the mystery!

Yes, experience has often led me to think that, if God did not exist, we should indeed be forced to invent him, since without him and what he represents we are not up to living and are in difficulty from our first cries or from our first steps. Without faith in God we are like someone trying to live in a roofless house, or trying to read at night without a lamp.

But God does not have to be invented. He is already invented, and is so near that we can feel his breath, when we are silent or when we pray.

Certainly problems of visibility exist. But these are not from his side, they are from our own infinite complications.

God is simple and we make him complicated. He is close to us and we think him far away. He is in the real and in events, and we look for him in dreams and impossible utopias.

The true secret of making contact with God is littleness, simplicity of heart, poverty of spirit: all the things that pride, wealth and cleverness foil in us.

Jesus has said it: '. . . unless you become like little children . . . you will never enter . . .' (Matthew 18:3), and he certainly was not joking or trying to have us on.

Whether or not we see God depends on our eye. If it is a simple eye, it sees him. If it is a baleful eye, it does not see him.

I had the good fortune to be born among the poor, among the marvellous folk of the countryside, who had simplicity and littleness kneaded into them. My father and mother were very little. They were just made for believing and hoping. And I found myself with my hand in their hands.

And everything was easier.

How at peace I felt with them, and how serene my childhood was!

It was like living within a great parable, where God was always at home and I was always with him. If, owing to distraction or frivolity, I sometimes forgot him, he always thought of a pain or a mystery to remind me of his presence.

But more than anything else, it was events that, very slowly, moulded everything together into one. To be sure, the mystery continued to surround me. In fact it became ever denser as I grew up and sought to understand.

The mystery! What was the mystery? It was like my mother's womb, hugging me all about, containing me and generating me to life, in that so discreet, sweet twilight under her heart.

What could be truer and simpler than a woman's womb, containing a child?

But what could be more mysterious and incomprehensible, if you set yourself to reasoning on the how, the why and the when?

Yes, the secret is to be little children!

In a child there is a basic intuition, given by God himself.

God gives human beings life, he gives them bread to sustain them – and he gives them this intuition, which is faith, to guide them and light their way.

And he gives it to all of them.

All of them!

He gives it not only to Jews and Christians, but to everyone, without exception.

He gave it to Paul when he said '. . . it is in him that we live, and move, and exist . . .' (Acts 17:28). He gave it to me, 2000 years after Paul. He gives it to the men and women who live in the tents of Islam. He gives it to the Hindus born on the banks of the Ganges, and to the Buddhists of Nepal and China.

God is the Catechist of the world, and his Spirit, who is Love, tears down every frontier, uniting the children he has created, since they are his and he cannot forget them.

As long as I have known God, I have known that he cannot forget us, and that he teaches us our catechism even if we live in a far-away land, where no missionary will ever come to speak to us of him.

Yes, God's catechism is simple, simple as he is, and it is basic for living as human beings and fulfilling ourselves in happiness. And it is in all of us.

You know how it goes:

- God is the Living, and the Good.
- God is the Beginning, and the End.
- All creation is a sign of him, but he is other than creation: he is the Transcendent One.
- The things of reality are his face and the testimony of his presence.
- God speaks to us through events, and history is our response to his word.

- God is eternal, and we are eternal with him.
- Love is the fullness of his law.
- Life tends towards resurrection, and the stages of death are passages, 'quantum leaps', 'thrusts', to grasp life completely. The more we die to ourselves the more we free ourselves from death.

Where is the problem then?

How is it possible not to believe? How is it possible not to accept the gift given by the Father who is God to his child who is the human being?

And yet John himself says that it is possible: 'He came to his own domain and his own people did not accept him' (John 1:11).

Yet, it is possible. It is possible not to accept God. But this does not depend on God. It depends on us.

We shall never be able to repeat this often enough. To accept him we have to be little children, and, more particularly, poor ones. After all, Jesus said that the good news was brought to the poor (Luke 4:18).

But here we must be clear about what we mean by being little, by being children. Do we mean immature cry-babies?

And what does being poor mean? Having your trousers in tatters, or being ill-housed?

Certainly not. And the Bible takes great care, all along its long way, to make us understand the meaning of these two words, words which are so vital to our relationship with God.

The 'little ones' are people who have no ultimate security, who are ever in search of their fulfilment in the reality surrounding them.

The 'poor' are those who do not transform the things they possess into idols – who feel deep down that nothing will satisfy them but the Absolute.

There is no way out. You see, the opposite of littleness is power, and the opposite of poverty is wealth.

Israel failed to understand Christ because it was caught in the snares of power; and the rich man did not follow Jesus, because he idolized his riches.

Some people may smile at such a simplification of today's tremendous problem of faith, surrounded as we are by a flood of atheism apparently swamping the whole world. And others may be taken aback by my statement that faith in God is given to all as an initial gift, like life, bread, breath.

I do not claim to speak persuasively. I seek to set forth, in simple terms, my own experience of God.

Each has his or her own path to follow.

There are those who see God as Creator.

There are those who know him as Being.

There are those who define him as the Architect of the world, the Unmoved Mover.

There are those who arrive at him by way of beauty, aesthetics, number, logic, the eternal, the infinite. And there are those who are aware of him as the Other, the Transcendent.

If I had to tell you what binds me to God, at the end of my earthly existence, I should say: all the paths listed above have helped me, and I have followed them now in one direction, now in another.

But what has helped me most, leading me out of 'systematic doubt', has been the experience of God.

When anyone asks me, especially after I have come back from the desert, 'Brother Carlo, do you believe in God?' I answer: 'Yes, I tell you in the Holy Spirit, I do believe.'

And if my questioner's curiosity is aroused, to the point of inquiring further: 'What evidence do you bring forward for asserting so great a truth?' I say, to conclude the conversation, 'Only this: I believe in God because I know him.'

I experience his presence in me twenty-four hours out of twenty-four. I know and love his word without ever questioning it. I am aware of his tastes and preferences, his way of speaking, and, especially, his will.

But here precisely, as regards knowing his will, is where things suddenly get difficult.

When I think that his will is Christ himself, and Christ's way of living and dying for love, I see him withdraw infinitely far from me.

God turns out to be far, far away. So far away, that he is inaccessible.

How could I ever live as Jesus lived?

How could I ever have the courage to suffer and die for love like Christ himself?

I who am so false, so unjust, so greedy, so fearful, so selfish, so proud?

How idle our prattle about 'believing' or 'not believing' in God!

Pure speculation, and more often than not, useless.

What counts is love, and we do not know how to love, or do not wish to.

Now I understand why Paul used such forceful language when he came to the heart of the matter, and explained to the Corinthians:

'If I have all the eloquence of men or of angels, but speak without love, I am simply a gong booming or a cymbal clashing.

'If I have the gift of prophecy, understanding all the mysteries there are, and knowing everything, and if I have faith in all its fullness, to move mountains, but without love, then I am nothing at all' (1 Corinthians 13:1–2).

Here is where the real problem lies. I run the risk of being a cipher, because I do not know how to love.

So stop asking yourselves whether you believe or do not believe in God. Ask yourselves whether you do or do not love.

And if you love, forget the rest. Just love.

And love ever more and more, to the point of folly – the true folly that leads to blessedness: the folly of the cross, which is the conscious gift of self, and which possesses the most explosive force imaginable for human liberation.

That love's folly passes by way of the discovery of one's own poverty, that real poverty of not knowing how to love, is a fact. But it is also a fact that when we reach that frontier impassable to man, all the creative power of God steps in, and he not only says:

'Now I am making the whole of creation new' (Revelation 21:5),
but adds:

'I shall remove the heart to stone from your bodies and give you a heart of flesh instead' (Ezekiel 36:26).

And thus, when we love, we experience God. We know God, and doubt disappears like mist in the sunshine.

2 Evil

If we could always remain children, little children in the Spirit, everything would be easier and faith in God would develop naturally, as a tree develops, containing the programme of its long future in its seed.

You see, there is something we must keep well in mind: It may be hard to believe, but it is a lot harder not to.

It is not easy to shrug off so colossal a thing as the whole universe with the simple phrase 'I don't believe', and blithely refuse all response to the tremendous logic of things visible.

Like it or not, faced with the real, I have to find a plausible reason for it – a reason that will satisfy my thirst to know.

After all, the real is there, right in front of me, with its life that I collide with, its light that envelops me, its love that seeks me out.

Saying 'I don't believe in God' ends up begging the question.

What if God were to be everything that is real? Could I deny him then, saying that he does not exist while I am actually seeing him, touching him, experiencing him?

Why not accept him?

Why not say yes to all that is visible?

Why not begin to fall in love with *that*? Why not go ahead and shout for joy at this reality clothed in light and flowers, and exult at its all-embracing might, and fall on my knees in ecstasy before its unutterable mystery?

Why not?

How many things it has to tell me, this All enfolding me, speaking to me through the alphabet of the stars, delighting me with its fantastic presence, always going before me and all but stifling me in the embrace of its infinitude and its all-enveloping unity!

Have today's human beings perhaps become more illogical then primitive man, who was so in love with the sun – adorable, fantastic thing that it is – that he made no bones about worshipping it?

Do today's human beings perhaps think they are 'smarter' by saying no to everything with their wiseacre sarcasm, and looking at everything with a jaundiced eye?

This is the one way never to succeed in arriving at the truth. This is the tried and true way of becoming deaf, dumb and blind, and staying that way.

I too could decide to stay on the outside. But it certainly would not be very interesting.

It would be boring, to say the least.

And certainly joyless and uncreative . . .

And so I have often wondered: Can it really be such a difficult thing to accept so simple a notion as the idea of God?

What is at the basis of this difficulty I have in saying yes, a yes shouted out by all things? What makes it so difficult to accept a simple logic that rules all logics – to make myself available to so evident and so universal a love?

It was in this difficulty that I then discovered a terrifying, inexorable presence – a presence dominating the whole universe, and present in each of us, deep within our spirit, in the hidden recesses of our soul.

When I thought about this, I felt that this presence had something of the implausible about it and that it was precisely behind its implausibility that it chooses to hide, the more easily to prevail.

Nor do I know what name to give to it, so as not to scandalize anyone or raise obstacles for anyone on the road to faith. When Paul VI made bold to refer to this presence, calling it Satan, many people were scandalized and accused him, the greatest and most prudent pope of our times, of reverting to the terrors and obscurantism of the Middle Ages.

Shall I call it the Evil One, the Tempter?

And why not call it Satan, as the gospel does (Matthew 12:26),

Beelzebul, as Jesus himself does (Matthew 12:27),
the devil (Matthew 4:5),
the unclean spirit (Luke 11:24),
the one who 'possesses', who takes over a person (John 8:48),
the liar (John 8:44),
the murderer, the one who brings death (John 8:44),
the prince of this world (John 12:31),
the reign of darkness (Luke 22:53)?

When Jesus challenged it to give its name, it replied: 'My name is . . . legion, for there are many of us' (Mark 5:9).

There is nothing more mysterious than the evil one.

But is God any less mysterious?

We ought to have the guts to accept a little of darkness, while keeping the wondering eye of surprised childhood fixed on that which is bright.

I do not seek to understand, I seek to believe.

I have not arrived at God by understanding, I have arrived at him by faith.

And Satan too. I do not understand him, I believe in him.

And just as it is in experience that I have received the answer of the existence of God, so it has been in experience that I have received the answer of the existence of Satan.

Perhaps it would be better not to call him Satan for the moment. Too many things pop into our mind. We are too spoiled by our mania for conjuring up pictures of things that cannot be pictured.

After all, Deuteronomy says (4:15–18): 'Take great care what you do, therefore . . . see that you do not act perversely, making yourselves a carved image in the shape of anything at all: whether it be in the likeness of man or of woman, or of any beast on the earth, or of any bird that flies in the heavens, or of any reptile that crawls on the ground, or of any fish in the waters under the earth.' Also: '. . . you saw no shape on that day at Horeb when Yahweh spoke to you from the midst of the fire . . .' (Deuteronomy 4:15).

I think the same goes for Satan, and I force myself to leave him behind the veil of mystery. Too readily have we drawn pictures of him, and in so doing have produced an irrational, distorted result.

Has he a face?

Is he without a face?

Has he a body?

Is he a spirit?

I do not know.

But I have learned to feel him, to experience him, and I cannot deny him. After all, the gospel does not deny him, and I am certainly not about to deny him.

I feel his presence as the Tempter.

How does he act? I do not know.

I only know that, as I look at human beings and their boundless abominations, it seems to me impossible for them to have managed to do such terrible things on their own.

Human beings are helped by someone else when they dig the abyss of sin in themselves, when they sink to the roots of despair.

There is someone behind them making suggestions when they deny truth and betray love.

There is someone supporting their arms when they hack their brothers and sisters to pieces by torture.

There is a sadistic spirit at hand, who stops at nothing, when a tyrant starves a people.

There is a planner when millions of people are gassed in extermination camps, and generations of children die of hunger under the indifferent eye of governments.

There is, there is, there is!

And there is one in us, too, when we no longer smile at life, when we have no more will to build, when we do not want a child, when we crowd the elderly into 'homes', when we hate our sister or our brother, when we are indifferent to someone's suffering, or when we fling ourselves on the ground and refuse to keep hoping.

And there is one in us when we stand before gleaming glaciers, or the trembling of the light upon the sea, and remain unmoved, empty of wonder.

And there is one in us when we ask the Real One surrounding us for his identity papers, and shout in his face: 'Who are you?

'Have you come to disturb us?' (cf. Mark 1:24).

After all, only I exist! I have no need of you!

I do not want you, God, because your power destroys mine, your will limits mine.

Yes, at bottom it is true, and the temptation of temptations is the one making me blaspheme in my madness: 'If you exist, then I cannot exist.'

Can I still be surprised if I find it hard to believe in God?

If so many people cry out in their foolishness, 'God does not exist'?

If my night is dark, if my heart is dry and knows not how to love?

If my hope droops and pales?

No, do not be astonished, my soul.

Do not be astonished if, to your timid, feeble yes, with which you seek to affirm the existence of God, the deafening answer of the Evil One comes crashing back in echo, 'No!'

No, he does not exist!

Do not be astonished if, in the face of your effort to fulfil yourself in truth and love, you feel him throw you to the ground, vanquished for the umpteenth time.

Do not be astonished if, in the face of your sincere promise to be faithful to man, you find yourself an hour later to be a two-faced traitor, a selfish, cruel, swaggering gangster and grafter.

Do not be astonished!

And do not be astonished either, when in prayer you hear the words of the Psalmist on your lips, 'So longs my soul for you, my God' (Psalm 42:2), and immediately afterwards you hear in reply:

'Where is your God?

'Where is your God?

'Where is your God?' (Psalm 42:4, 10).

Yes, the Evil One, the Tempter, is like the proliferation of a cancer inside me, spreading, developing wherever it possibly can, seeking to destroy everything within me, right to the roots.

There. Perhaps the comparison with a cancer is the most apt one, the most appropriate 'sign' of evil personalized in Satan: of that tremendous reality that has impressed the generations, continuously being accepted or rejected, impossible to define in its mysterious, yet genuine and indisputable, presence.

Yes, evil is within me and I cannot deny it.

Sometimes it is so embedded in me, so identified with my own reality, that I can no longer distinguish it in its essence.

Am I a 'cancer' unto myself? Or is it a cancer I can excise with a scalpel and get rid of?

Usually I perceive it as something other than myself, and I give it a name, as the gospel gives it a name, and I fight it as a mortal enemy.

It is a mysterious thing, and I prefer to take Jesus' word for it and not discuss it too much. Otherwise I become lost in the maze of my own reasoning and fail to reach a conclusion.

But there is one thing I do know about it, something I know from experience. I know that it always attacks me at my central part, at my relationship with God, trying to destroy that relationship, trying to destroy what unites me with him . . . faith, hope, charity.

It is a continual, life-and-death struggle, and I have never seen my poverty to be so real as in this combat.

This is why I feel pity for myself, and pity for all who claim not to believe or find it hard to believe.

I know what that means.

I feel, too, that when the churches insist so much on moral codes and take so much interest in listing the various 'legal' sins and getting them confessed, they do not realize they are putting a sticking-plaster over a wound, the deepest wound of all.

No, my friends, the real sin we should confess, and should confess every day, especially today, is our
'not believing,
'not hoping,
'not loving'.

We have never sufficiently bewailed our weakness in faith, in hope and in charity, and we have never sufficiently noticed the presence of the Evil One in this struggle of ours.

Another thing that the spirit of evil seeks to do is to divide up my unity and to set me at odds with myself.

This is why he is called the divider.

When prophecy proclaims a truth about God to me, using the actual, real me, I immediately deny it.

When I find myself with Abraham at the terebinth of Mamre, and the angel comes to say that Sarah will have a child, when I know that Sarah is sterile and old, I feel, rising within me, Sarah's laughter behind the tent-flap as she thinks 'It is not possible' (cf. Genesis 18).

Woe to me if God were to hear and keep account of all the times that Sarah laughs within me!

'. . . God created the heavens and the earth' (Genesis 1:1).

And Sarah laughs, because it does not seem a likely thing to her.

'The Word was made flesh' (John 1:14).

And Sarah stands before the mystery of the God made visible on earth in Christ, and laughs.

'. . . this is my body . . . this is my blood . . .' (Matthew 26:26, 28), and the laughter goes on.

Here truly is the nature of evil, in the ability to say no to faith, to hope, to love.

This is the sin in which we are immersed to the tops of our heads.

This is the sin I confess every day, and which every day springs up in me anew.

This is my poverty.

This is our true poverty.

This is our sorrow.

This is our weakness.

So you see, I have not escaped this painful reality; and after a placid, unruffled childhood, lived as it were for free in the bosom of my family, I went through an adolescence marked by the struggle with doubt and by the enfeebling of hope.

Uneasiness was born in me, and the dying away of joy became ever more noticeable.

I came to know things forbidden, and their mysterious attraction.

My mother started telling me not to turn in on myself so much, and would complain about my selfishness.

On occasion, when looking in the mirror, I discovered my capacity for sarcasm.

In my heart, I revolted more and more.

My family had less and less influence over me.

Alone, I was reeling.

And then it was that the Church came to meet me.

As the family is the first great aid and support of our first steps, so the Church is the aid and support of all our steps, especially in the struggle against evil.

What would the family be without the community formed by the Church?

What would Israel be without the people of God?

Someone once made a very true and intelligent observation: 'You will find peoples without city walls, and without art. But you will never find a people without a temple.'

My own first temple was the parish church, which welcomed the big boy I was, the teenager in crisis, the little one in evolution, like an antenna receiving signals from all the beautiful and not so beautiful realities of street, school, factory, shops – from the human community in which I was immersed.

How extraordinary the parish church is! Even when it is a twisted, poor, old-fashioned house as mine was!

We had not reached the Council yet, and the parish church was still a sacrament-dispensing machine and a big hodge-podge of childishness and clericalism.

But it was the meeting-place of the people of God, and what human beings did not do, the power of the Spirit and common faith did.

I may have had little faith, but the faith of others met me along the way; unedifying examples there may have been in abundance, but the great examples of the poor, of the simple, and of the holy priests, were never lacking.

How I loved and love the parish church, even though I often hid myself behind the pillars supporting the nave in order to avoid my responsibilities.

The parish church is like a ship at sea, a calm in the woods, a shelter in the mountains. It has always something to offer, even when old and often without form or beauty.

I breathed a tradition, even if a little musty; I absorbed a culture, a bit static though it may have been; I found a people, even if they were sometimes rather tired.

What the parish church has been for our peoples!

What the parish church has been for the Irish, the Italians, the Poles!

But here, too, there is another step that has to be taken.

Let me explain.

3 The Saving Community

On my last trip to Australia, I encountered an almost universal complaint on the part of priests (and not only of priests): 'We are suffering a serious leakage of Catholics to the Jehovah's Witnesses. And the strange thing is that it strikes the very ones who are most religious.'

To those who questioned me about this phenomenon, so rife among the Italian immigrants, I made bold to reply that there was nothing strange about it at all, and that it would continue, and worsen, unless . . .

. . . Unless we were to change our system, we who belong to great Churches rich in tradition and walls: colossal walls, walls incurring the risk of sclerosis or of giving the impression of having nothing inside.

For me it is in no way strange if people from the Abruzzi or from Sicily, rich in religious feeling and acutely homesick, finding themselves lost in a huge country where they have come in search of work, feel the cold on entering a great, anonymous Church where they know no one, where relationships are collective rather than personal, and where it is very difficult to re-construct unity and intimacy.

The least that can happen is that they will go through a crisis.

And if, in that crisis, they are approached by a Jehovah's Witness, or a member of some other militant religious sect who invites them home and in some modest place introduces them to a group of believers who pray side by side, who know one another's names, who share their goods . . . and especially, who place them, for the first time in their lives, before a mysterious, solemn book that until now they have known only as a name – the 'Bible' – and teach them how to handle it and to look up page, chapter and verse . . .

. . . Victory is theirs. The immigrant will go home and tell his or her family, 'I have found real sisters and brothers', and slowly, slowly, become detached from his or her tired old roots.

It is precisely the thirst for the Church that drives men and women, especially the poorest of them, to look for a Church.

But a Church to the measure of their poverty and their needs.

The great, official, solemn Church, replete with ceremony, with visible power, with numbers, no longer impresses.

Today's people, knowing the anguish of loneliness, want a Church made of friendship, of genuine contacts, of mutual interchange, of little things.

But more than anything else, a Church that feeds them with the Word, a Church that works with them by physically taking them by the hand, a Church whose face is like that of the Church of Luke, of Mark, of John, a Church that is just starting, a Church . . . that smells of beginnings.

Yes, this is why our Italian immigrant in Australia, almost in spite of himself, abandons his roots.

This is always unlovely and often traumatic.

If, instead of a Jehovah's Witness, our immigrant had met a Focolarino, a member of a Neo-Catechumenal Way community, a militant of Catholic Action, a member of Renewal in the Spirit, or (if a youngster) a Catholic Scout . . . things would have turned out differently.

These kinds of Christians would have invited him, not to the forbidding parish church, but to their own little meeting-place, poor, yet warm in affection and rich in personal relationship.

No one wants to switch Churches if their own Church offers what they seek and thirst for: truth, love, friendship, personal relationship.

In my own case, the little church that helped me understand

the big Church and remain in it, was the Youth Movement of Catholic Action.

It took me by the hand and walked with me, it fed me with the Word, it offered me friendship, it taught me how to fight, it helped me know Christ, it inserted me alive into a living reality.

I can say – and this seems to me to be the correct way of putting it – that just as the family was the spring, so the little youth community was the riverbed in which I learned to swim.

What a help this community was to me!

And what would have become of me if I had not found it?

I tremble at the very thought.

It gave me just what my parents, who were growing old now, could no longer give me . . .

Catholic Action made me undergo a new catechesis: a more mature one, more in keeping with the times. It passed on to me the great idea of the lay apostolate; it introduced the Church to me as the people of God and not as the familiar, old-fashioned clerical pyramid.

But even more, it gave me the feeling and warmth of community.

For me, the Church was no longer the walls of the parish church, where you went to do obligatory or official things, but a community of brothers known to one another by name, who were travelling with me along the road of faith and love.

There I came to know friendship based on common faith, and commitment to a common task that was no longer the prerogative of the clergy but a gift given to all. I came to know the dignity of working and raising a family as a genuine vocation.

Little by little the community helped me to take on my responsibilities, suggested to me my first commitments and encouraged me in them, taught me how to publish newsletters and write in defence of the faith, and gave me a taste for the Word and taught me to proclaim it at meetings.

And, since I was untrained, the community was always careful to instil in me the humility of study, and daily meditation on the Scriptures.

After a few years I found I had changed. Now my heart was filled with new values and a great desire for action.

I remember, there was no more spare time. Between personal contacts and first drafts of speeches, between writing and travelling, my entire personality was caught up, completely caught up, in an ideal that had now taken flesh in real life.

Today, some official ministers, especially parish priests and bishops, are surprised, and often perplexed, at the proliferation of the so-called movements or prayer groups or spirituality groups. Some of them, lacking experience with this phenomenon, and surprised that anything good can arise outside the realm of officialdom, go so far as to place obstacles and prohibitions in the way of these movements, seeing in them only their defects and especially a weakening of the parish and its unity.

If these zealous shepherds were not in good faith, they would merit a harsh judgement indeed – which I do not pronounce, but which you can find by looking in the gospel, for it was pronounced by Jesus himself.

Because . . . neither did Jesus have the permission of officialdom to start what he wanted to start.

But I do not wish to become involved in polemics.

I shall content myself merely with saying that the birth of the movements today (and I shall put a short list of them in a note, so as not to interrupt our train of thought) is prodigious proof of the action of the Holy Spirit, and one of the most effective means by which he sows the seeds of tomorrow.[1]

The birth of these communities – almost all of them

1 Here are a few: Communauté chrétienne de formation française (founded 1974); L'Arche (France, 1964); Comunione e liberazione (Italy, 1954); Comunità dirita cristiana (new name of the Marian Congregations); Cultura y Fe (Brazil, 1976); Cursillos de Cristianidad (Spain, 1949); Eau Vive (France, 1967); Teams of Our Lady (France, 1939); Light and Life (Poland, 1964); Movimento Chiesa-Mondo (Italy, 1976); Focolare Movement (Italy, 1943); Oasis (Italy, 1950); Catholic Charismatic Renewal (United States, 1967); Schoenstatt Foundation (Germany, 1914); Sodalitium Christianae Vitae (Peru, 1971); Christ–Communion–Liberation (Uganda, 1970); Pro Sanctitate (Italy, 1947); Living Church (Czechoslovakia, 1964).

founded on a more intimate quest for the Word, on a burning desire for communion, on a more modern redistribution of charisms and evangelical tasks – is the sign of the need to spread efficacious faith and love through all parts of the Church, so as to restore the old structure to youth and vital strength.

One thing is certain, and visible to all: the development of this phenomenon has been prodigious. It is a sign of the vitality of Christianity today, and a response to a genuinely felt need.

If I were a parish priest today, I would not try to block these spirituality movements or these 'spontaneous communities', for fear that 'something might happen'. No, I should make an effort to foster and encourage them, so that every Christian might have the opportunity and feel the attraction of getting involved and of travelling with whatever group is best equipped to draw this particular person out of his or her solitude. But above all I should be at pains to see that the groups be based on the great ruling ideas of the Church today:

- Evangelization,
- The journey of faith,
- Prayer,
- The sharing of goods.

There is no point in wasting time in a discussion of the defects that here appear. The Focolarini 'smile too much'; the Neo-Catechumenal Way communities shut themselves up in a 'ghetto', and have their 'own liturgy'; the Scouts 'waste their time pitching tents in the woods', far from the parish, when there is such a need for catechists; the Comunione e liberazione people are too involved with 'the world'.

Yes, all this may be true. No movement is without its defects. But – strangely – they are alive. They have the thrust and strength of ideals, they grow – you see them – they get involved, and . . . they do not go over to the Jehovah's Witnesses.

The only movement exhibiting no defects at all is the one blessed with all the chrisms of officialdom. It has no defects, but is dead – or, if not dead, is so sombre and boring that its membership is restricted to those who have to be there to avoid offending someone.

I have to own that, in these stormy years, the ones who have given me comfort as Church, have been precisely the movements and communities. I have seen them by the hundreds and thousands, and for me they represent the true marching wing of the Church.

In the Middle Ages, Francis founded the Franciscans and Dominic the Dominicans. Today, Chiara Lubich has founded the Focolare, Chico Arguello the Neo-Catechumenal Way, and Edoardo Bonin the Cursillos de Cristianidad. And these are certainly no less considerable in capacity and scope.

What strength, what initiative, in the basic Christian communities! Go to Brazil and see what is happening in the thousands of basic communities there, scattered among the poor in the vast countryside and the shanty-towns. You will be speechless with admiration.

Have you ever taken part in a Cursillo weekend? You will emerge inside-out and upside-down, having rediscovered the meaning of true conversion.

Have you ever been to a Focolare meeting in Germany, Italy, Japan or Hong Kong? Spend an evening there. You will understand why too many religious of either sex are sad and melancholy in their communities, while here they are bursting with joy and vitality.

Have you ever had the luck to spend the Easter Vigil with a Neo-Catechumenal Way community, after sharing the fast in which all have prepared for the explosive singing of the *Exultet*, announcing the Passover of the Lord?

If you have had that experience, you will no longer have any wish to go and take part in a service celebrated in the coldness and indifference of an uncatechized, official, formal congregation.

Have you ever gone out one spring morning before school to recite Lauds with a throng of Comunione e Liberazione people?

Or got into a bus and found a girl from the Sant'Egidio community sitting next to you, happily telling you about her satisfaction in working for the elderly, or for young runaways in a poor quarter of the city?

Have you ever squeezed into a crowd of charismatics at prayer, praying the whole night through in an atmosphere electric with the fire of the presence of the Spirit?

For me these things have always been among my most beautiful religious experiences, in my journeys across the world.

Emerging from these gatherings, I never felt like wondering whether good or evil was winning in the world of today, or whether we have cause to be pessimistic about spiritual realities and the vitality of the Church.

Bless you, communities of prayer and faith!

Bless you, communities of commitment and life!

For me you recall the primitive communities from which Christianity was born – the communities of Luke, Matthew and James, of Paul and Diognetus.

Communities which fed on the Word of God, and proclaimed the good news to the poor.

Bless you, communities of love, that seek to follow Jesus' gospel, communities I do not yet know, and perhaps never shall know, for I am old and weary – but communities which, by your presence and witness, give such joy to my life.

No one reminds me of my youth as you do, of my first days in the apostolate, of the nights under the stars when I cycled home from a meeting of some group – one of the many communities then being founded everywhere in the great suburbs. You see, the Church was not my only group. It was as if a fire were spreading all over the surface of the earth.

Bless you.

Bless you.

Bless you.

One final word to those who would like to know more – to those who are in the habit of discerning tomorrow in spiritual phenomena and of perceiving the mysterious path of the Church in the world through the testimony of individuals.

This is a method much used today, especially by the movements. If you go to a Mariapolis or take part in an adult

Catholic Action meeting, in whatever country you please, you will be convinced at once.

This is the way the Spirit acts today, and anyone who has schooled himself to see the invisible in the human can feel the warmth of the fire creeping through the stubble of the field, and of the conflagrations here and there as the Spirit wills.

I was telling you how, in the past, the people of God founded orders and 'spiritualities'. Today we have the same thing; and very simple but extremely alive and attentive men and women are founding movements and setting spiritualities afoot which are producing a tremendous result and which truly have the power to proclaim the Good News with effective words and methods.

It might seem strange, and for some it may be disedifying . . . but among the hierarchy, nothing of this is going on at all, and I mean absolutely nothing.

I must admit I have had to meditate a lot before grasping the meaning of this fact.

When I was young and immature, I was puzzled. Now that I am old, I am convinced.

It came to me like a bolt of lightning in my riper years.

It is not the hierarchy's business to make new foundations. New foundations have already been raised on the eternal foundation: Christ.

The bishops have no need to found a spirituality. They are the guarantors of the spirituality which is at the very root of the Church: Jesus crucified and risen.

The Church is like an oak, and the hierarchy is like its trunk. New foundations, the manner in which one expresses oneself at a given time, variations, expansion to win life and give oxygen, reside in the branches, in the leaves. All is harmonious, and Jesus himself made this comparison, with the image of the vine and the branches (cf. John 15:5).

It is true, I said to myself, the hierarchy in my time has founded nothing, absolutely nothing. But it has given me the gift of something which in force and solidity may equal everything that has ever been founded, and may even surpass it. It has given me the gift of the Council, which is the manner in which the Church today expresses its reality, its spirituality, its proclamation, its stability, its indissoluble, unshakable unity, its deepest strength.

When I look at the Council, I feel like a leaf in comparison with the trunk. I feel like a little berry as compared with the whole. I feel *in* the Church today.

Archbishop Lefebvre does not make me angry for wanting to go on saying Mass in Latin, any more than my grandfather made me angry when he always wanted his same cup at table, and woe betide anyone who switched on him! It is a question of old age (today spitefully called sclerosis). He makes me angry because he speaks ill of the Council, and this for me is an offence against the faith we ought to have in the Church alive today.

Well, then, speaking of the Council, what shall we make of all these branches that have come out of the trunk, this infinity of movements, new foundations and communities, too numerous to count – as it used to be said in fun of congregations of sisters that only the Holy Spirit knew how many of them there were?

Yes, it is hard to count leaves, and if you want some advice, Your Excellencies, do not count them.

Let them sprout. If they are of the Spirit, they will grow; if not, they will die of themselves.

Do not go about with a hatchet and surly look, ferreting out novelty. Be concerned instead with spreading plenty of good fertilizer under the tree, the fertilizer of the Word of God, and know that yourselves are not the ones to change things.

Your job is different! Know, rather, something that I consider basic in these times of rebirth, of the Church-tree's springtime.

Your task is to relate multiplicity to unity. This is the mission of the tree-trunk, the mission of the hierarchy.

When I was a boy and first entered church life, I recall my astonishment at never seeing a Franciscan arm-in-arm with a Dominican, or a Conventual conversing with a Capuchin.

That was the way it was.

But the strange thing is that it is still that way today, though on other levels.

If the Focolare hold a convention on the spirituality of marriage, you can rest assured you will never see anyone from Comunione e Liberazione there. By the same token, if Comunione e Liberazione tries to set up an apostolate in a university, you can be very certain that it will not be able to count on the basic Christian communities or Catholic Action.

There is nothing new under the sun, and though the Church may be having a reawakening, the Evil One is having a reawakening too and will try to divide, to weaken and to slander God and his works.

Isn't this so?

Third: I venture to tell you that this is a time for great humility and infinite patience. When life bursts forth, with all the force of modern methods, we must be more far-sighted, more generous and more committed than ever to that basic witness which, after all, is the witness that Jesus imparts to us.

And besides, if we wish to emulate Pope Roncalli in one of his concerns, we shall have to keep an eye on the signs of the times.

What does all this mean?

In pedestrian language, if I were a bishop, I should keep account of two things, which follow from all we have said here. They may be expressed in two very simple words: multiplicity and unity.

I would not panic at the first of these. I should not get into the habit of saying no to people's attempts to get together in the diocese. Rather, I should concern myself with very slowly and patiently building up lines of communication leading sooner or later to the unity of the whole.

And this means: a right to live for the movements, and a concern to give the laity a training for unity in a conscientious, humble, extremely mature and respectful Catholic Action.

I do not like it when a shepherd says: 'I'm in charge in this diocese. No movements! If you want a movement, you can have Catholic Action and that's it.'

Just as I do not like it when a bishop relies exclusively on movements and considers Catholic Action a thing of the past.

Both are needed. Movements are vessels for the breath of the Spirit animating the Church and giving it freedom to develop and worship the various mysteries of Christ, while Catholic Action, grafted directly on to the hierarchy, is the vehicle for the charism of leading the parts to unite and love the Body of Jesus, that is to say, the Church.

There is nothing new under the sun.

And as, yesterday, it was the religious congregations that flourished, with all their differing spiritualities, and the bishops unified them all in the project known as Church Universal, so today, under the same impulse, it is the movements that flourish and increasingly feel the need for a Catholic Action capable of expressing, in the immense forum of the laity, the hierarchy's concerns about safeguarding unity and communion among the members of the Mystical Body of the Church.

Not for nothing did the Second Vatican Council make a point of commending Catholic Action, which remains, even if you were to change its name or make use of another 'instrument', the expression of a truly universal and irreplaceable idea in the Church.

On that foundation of unity, of which the hierarchy alone are guarantors, since possessing the charism bestowed on them by Jesus himself, each of us can build our own house, or hermitage, or monastery, or convent or group.

All in the freedom of the children of God.

And this is no small thing.

4 Oh, That You Were My Sister!

I have always been in love with everything. Imagine, then, how it was when it came to women! For me the beauty that packed creation was a mighty summons to communication and joy.

My heart has never been empty and dry.

As a boy I played like crazy, and to be sweaty and happy to be alive was the norm.

Later on I played the piano and fell in love with that, to the point of becoming an occasion of distress to neighbours, harried by my persistence.

Then it was colours that became objects of my love, and there were horrible paintings I had daubed, even hanging in the cellar.

When I was introduced to the Youth Movement of Catholic Action and began to assimilate some of its ideals, which in those days we called the apostolate, I wanted to change the world in the space of a single generation – mine.

My love for woman was the background of my whole life and the sustained note of my existence. At times it impassioned me, at times it made me melancholic, but it was always there as an irreplaceable harmonic in the unity of the whole.

My first love was Pierina. I was eleven.

The only thing I remember about her is her name. Not even her face has stayed with me. I had seen her only a few times – but this was not important, since love is born in obscurity and does not need much light or many tokens.

She, Pierina, was present only in mystery to me, as I daydreamed about her in the streets of an outlying working-class district where my family was then living.

They were only dreams, and so, naturally, her memory faded.

The name remained, through time prolonging the emotion I felt when pronouncing it: Pierina.

At fourteen, woman's space within me was occupied by a little girl called Ninetta.

I used to see her in the playground behind the parish church, on our way to catechism.

I recall, she had curly hair. Once I lightly touched her shoulder. Not by accident, either.

My fingers can still feel the softness of that feminine body, but as something far, far away and more shrouded in mystery than ever.

I did not see her again. My family moved into the city, where my father had found accommodation in a housing co-operative.

In the city, I quickly fell in love with Vittorina, who lived on the top floor of the building where my family had gone to live. She went to school, played the piano and had long, long tresses.

It seems it was all too obvious that I was in love and was wasting too much time looking up at the third floor. Instead of meeting her in the street, as I very much wanted to, I met her mother – who told me very kindly that I was young, that I ought to keep up with my studies, and that her daughter ought to study too.

That meeting was quite a cold shower. And as I was a disciplined boy, from that day forward I understood that to love a girl was a family affair, and that I should have realized this.

And I should have realized first of all about mothers, who were extremely watchful and alert.

And, indeed, my special interest in the presence of mothers in my love affairs dates from then.

Meanwhile I had reached eighteen and become an elementary-school teacher in a country village.

As I often went to church, I naturally fell in love in church. She was a thin, frail little creature, all eyes, silence and melancholy. She belonged to a very wealthy, arrogant family – a misfortune for a dreamer like her – Ada!

In spite of my lack of initiative, poor little country-school teacher that I was, Ada herself took an interest in me, and the mere thought that a woman could think about me gave me no choice.

I would have done anything she had asked me.

But she did not ask me to do anything. Because her mother stepped in. Her mother was the kind who would patrol the family ricefields herself, and word was that when a strike was on she never went out without her leggings and pistol.

When this woman observed that her daughter was in love with an elementary-school teacher, she shut her up at home, and did all she could to ruin her already delicate health.

I never saw Ada again, and even though the thought of her filled me with anguish, I made a point of keeping well out of the way.

This was the first time I was hurt by the arrogance of wealthy families who regard love as a family and financial arrangement. It was unseemly for a rich heiress to marry a poor elementary-school teacher.

I had to come to grips with this, even though I had not been the prime mover.

Ada's ill-health made me ill myself, and her doctor told me she spent her time reading sentimental novels and pining away from nostalgia and loneliness, such being the fashion then, as from a subtle disease.

Ada never got well, and this drama, little as I may have provoked it myself, scarred me for years, interiorizing my love to depths I had never known were there.

Woman appeared to me more and more as a mysterious, delicate jewel-case, worthy to be touched with flowers, and caressed in dreams.

A year later, I was in the army in Milan, a cadet at the Alpine Military Academy.

Barracks were anything but the ideal surroundings for thinking about women in the way to which I was accustomed. Quite the reverse!

I could not bear the scurrility and filth with which love was discussed.

And here I must say something not without relevance to social training. Instead of making me give in, this all too general loose talk about love sharpened my inner need and determination to beat another path for myself and, more than anything else, confirmed for me the primacy of chastity over the irrationality of lust.

Love treated in this way only enhanced the dream I had constructed about woman, and the encounter with all that sewage, of which the barracks seemed to be the sump, convinced me of the beauty of self-giving and true love.

Then something happened that explained to me how even evil can help us along our road.

A friend in my squad who had just received his law degree, invited the whole company out to dinner to celebrate.

I had been along, and now I was walking back to barracks, with some of the others, through the Milanese fog, after a very pleasant meal in a restaurant.

At this point, one of the guests proposed we pay a visit to an aunt, who, he said, lived in the neighbourhood and would pop a cork for us to crown the feast.

But the story about the aunt and the wine had only been invented for me – I being the only practising Christian in the group – so as not to alarm me, and to make me compromise my principles.

I still recall the hallway, the stairs, the glass door with the light streaming through.

Suddenly I could feel a certain oddness in the situation, underscored by the strange smiles of my companions. But I was so naive that I still did not know what was happening to me!

Great was the others' glee when, without my knowing what had happened, there I was in a house of prostitution!

I tried to think what else it might be. But the scene before my eyes was such as to remove all doubt. I blushed to the roots of my hair and turned to face the soldier who had played the joke on me. He was laughing. I sank my fist in his stomach and flung the door open with such violence that I shattered the glass in it.

I flew down the stairs and out once more into the Milanese fog. I felt like screaming and crying.

Back in barracks, I remember, the slender figure of Ada came to my mind, and stayed: Ada lying on a chaise-longue in her garden. And men seemed to me like soldiers of fortune, incapable of grasping the need for a love too big for their arrogant passions.

No, for me, women were something else. And I thank God for having explained this so well to me.

When I was twenty-three and God burst in on me with his Spirit, my new relationship with him radically changed my life.

Everthing was new now and everything was influenced by the change that followed my conversion.

And first and foremost the problem of women.

Thus the problem of femininity became the precise line of force along which God strode towards me to explain himself to me and introduce me to the mystery of things invisible.

God came in as lover.

At first this seemed so beautiful, so warm, that I thought it must be sentimental presumption on my part. I was almost afraid to define it. I was frightened of falling victim to an over-facile, over-cultivated romanticism.

But it was none of this.

The intimacy God bestowed on me was so true, so strong, that it left its tokens and left them where there could be no room for doubt: in life, in sorrow, in joy, in conversation with my fellow-men, in the raw task of every day.

If he held me in his arms, I could spend the whole night in prayer. If he spoke to me, it was easy to forgive someone who had done me wrong. If he stopped in my room, I would have gone to the ends of the earth for the gospel he preached.

I shall never forget the manner in which his Spirit burst in on me.

He stormed in like someone madly in love and asked me to love him back with total madness of my own.

And there was something here that removed all doubt, that wiped out my suspicion that the encounter could be mere emotionalism, that convinced me that this was for real, and that this tremendous love was something altogether different from fantasy – that it was the Word of God.

In the Word, I found all that I had felt, explained. I found the key to the wonderful castle which I had now entered, without knowing how.

I learned Hosea by heart. With Ezekiel, I wept for my betrayals of love. I hoped against hope with Isaiah, and my story took flesh in the story of Israel.

Yes, it was indeed Israel, who was a man and who had been called Jacob before his 'passage', a cunning man, able to stand up to anyone at any time, no matter whom, even God, to be really true to himself – it was indeed Israel who changed my name too, and taught me that, in reality, man on earth was a woman and the one true spouse was God alone.

At first it struck me as strange that God should address Israel in the feminine: 'I shall make you my bride for ever' (Hosea 2:21); but then, in the light of experience, I grasped that this was exactly the way things really are: that God addresses each of us, even the men, in the feminine.

The Church is feminine, the people of God is feminine.

Israel is feminine.

My human nature is feminine.

When I say to the Lord 'I love you', I am speaking to him as to my bridegroom, and when I am at home with him I cuddle up close, like a little girl who expects everything from him and has no desire to show how smart she is.

Just like a bride. Or, better, like a woman in love, since the marriage is consummated only after the Apocalypse.

The whole spirituality of biblical man is femininity, passivity, availability, expectation, quest for littleness, service, adoration.

If you do not believe this, or if you are surprised at what I say, read the Prophets, and you will no longer have any doubt.

Israel's grand intuition, which runs throughout the Old

Testament and is the joy of the people of God, is precisely the intuition that God is her bridegroom.

This is the source of her strength and her glory.

Listen to these extraordinary words of Isaiah: 'Like a young man marrying a virgin, so will the one who built you wed you . . .' (Isaiah 62:5).

And this is really the way it is.

This is a fact.

This is the synthesis of the whole mystical life.

But this reality, this synthesis, is not something having to do with a single category of men or women, people who have taken the vow of chastity, as we say – as is sometimes thought in the Church.

Nothing could be more absurd.

This reality, this type of relationship, concerns everyone, married or not. It concerns John, who was a virgin, and it concerns David, who was not. It concerns Paul, the great defender of celibacy, and it concerns Abraham, who among other things had two wives. It concerns my brother the Bishop, and it concerns my mother who brought me into the world.

In the mystical life, which is the most intimate relationship possible between man and God, the Word uses marriage precisely because marriage is the type of relationship most suitable for explaining things; it is the type of relationship that is the most passionate, the most giving and the most free.

And, I might add, the most true.

What occurs between God and me on this earth, as the beginning, and in the Kingdom, as the end, is that perfect union, of which marriage is the most exact, most comprehensive sign.

Union in life.

Union in truth.

Union in will.

Union in tastes and pleasures.

Union in language.

Union of home.

Union at table.
Union in fertility.
Union in joy.
Union in the Everlasting.
It is indeed a marriage, and it is universal.
It is not about the body, it is about the being.
It is not about the senses, it is about the person.
It is not about the contingent, it is about the absolute.
It is not about emotionalism, it is about love.
It is not about weakness, it is about the will.
It is the marriage of heaven and earth.
Of the visible and the invisible.
It is God with us.
It is the Kingdom.
It is paradise.
It is the union of all things.

But to get back to women! I originally intended to call this chapter 'My Women'.

I finally gave it a title taken from the Song of Songs: 'Oh, that you were my sister . . .' (cf. Song of Songs 8:1). Well, it really says 'that you were my brother', but it is no disloyalty to the meaning of the verse if I address woman with the words the bride in the Song addresses to her Bridegroom. And the verse goes on, '. . . I could kiss you without people being shocked'.

When I reached maturity in life and the path of faith led me to the Song of Songs, woman returned to my horizon.

And she returned because I offered her to the Absolute of God.

I was then thinking about getting married: the thought had not even occurred to me that there might be any other choice.

I wanted to get married, I dreamed of getting married, I was happy when I thought about being married.

And instead . . .

It happened one afternoon. It was hot on account of the sirocco blowing across the city.

I was kept waiting by a doctor friend of mine, who was held up at the hospital. We had planned to go for a walk along the Po and talk about our common ideals for changing the world – immediately . . . as happens when you are young and still unaware of the actual problems.

I went into a church, to calm the tumultuous thoughts burning inside me, and sat down quite close to the tabernacle. I felt the refreshing coolness filling the great nave, but closed my eyes because everything was ugly, old and slovenly.

For some time then I had been in the habit of keeping my eyes closed when I prayed, and seeking more for peace than words, more for the Presence than formal worship.

There I was, sitting, when . . .

Yes, when the unforeseeable happened.

I had often read in the Bible about Abraham's encounter at the terebinth of Mamre.

Was my encounter of the same nature?

I do not know.

Did I recall the burning bush seen by Moses?

Was it the same thing?

I cannot tell . . .

I had often thought of the touch of Someone who knocks on your door, calling your name, as happened to Samuel, and you feel like saying 'Lord, what can I do for you?'

It was like this, but different – impossible to put such things into words.

I know that this unforeseeable 'passage' left me with something very clearly and precisely new: an altogether unfamiliar proposal, the beginning of a personal, particularly challenging and warm, conversation.

You will not marry.

You will stay single.

I shall be with you.

Do not be afraid.

In the days that followed, it was easy to see that things had changed in me and that the passage of God had been a radical one. I had the palpable conviction that I would now no longer be able to fall in love in a certain way with a woman, and that if I wanted to be happy, I should have to remain single.

Alone with my God.

Furthermore, I understood that I would no longer be able

to say 'yes' to a woman. I felt I would have deserted her halfway down the road and that my own route was marked out in advance. I had no option.

Frankly, I have to say that I did not look for other options: I was so happy, and the kind of intimacy with which God had willed to bind my heart to his mystery, gave me such joy.

Yes, God had asked me not to marry. He had asked that, of all things, of me, who had always been in love. And he had asked it so clearly that there could be no doubt about it.

I loved to re-read salvation history with this new secret of mine, and I must admit I felt heaven to be nearer.

How struck I was, as I meditated on the biblical passage where God asks Jeremiah not to take a wife, so that his loneliness will be a sign of the total self-giving required by the Absolute.

I have to tell you, though, that I felt luckier than Jeremiah. Yes, luckier than Jeremiah. And I knew why, too.

Jeremiah had not known Christ, and virginity in the Old Testament was much more burdensome than in the New.

The Good News of the Kingdom had not yet come.

For me, the loneliness of heart that God asked of me was nothing but joy, deep, true joy.

It has never been a burden for me to stay alone with God.

The thought of being with him, alone, without intermediaries, I have never found anything but uplifting.

What a sublime adventure, celibacy on this earth!

It is the true sign of the last times.

It is the door of the Apocalypse.

It is the nightwatch of the Bridegroom.

When I realize this, I feel the thrill of things divine.

And so where has woman ended up for me?

Is she absent from my consecrated life?

What sorrow would be mine!

No, celibacy does not justify the absence of woman, any more than living alone justifies the absence of flowers in my garden and fresh water in my fountain.

No, this is not what God has asked of me: the exclusion from my love of half the human race.

It has always pained me when religious men, seized with terror at the danger they incur through woman's presence, throw up walls and build impenetrable screens. And worse, close their hearts.

This is the easier way, suitable for those who are childish in their faith – and, I must add, often valuable too, since recommended by holy and wise men, no less.

For myself, I have never liked 'for men only', or 'for women only', for aesthetic reasons if for no other.

I did my best not to go off to a seminary, and today, when I go to a city to evangelize, I always prefer to stay with a family, even a noisy one, rather than with a stiff and severe community 'for men only'.

It is a matter of taste, I have to admit.

But to get back to the subject. Has woman shown up again in my existence?

How could she not, if I wanted to be part of the Church and live in the Church?

How could I shut out half the human race? And how could I dismiss the possibility of loving so many sublime creatures?

Because, I really mean it, they were sublime, or certainly seemed so to me.

In parish life the most vivacious, in communities the most faithful, in evangelization the most conscientious, in cordiality the most affable, in self-giving the most generous.

No, I could not shut them out! And I have not shut them out.

What is more, I have loved them.

With them everything has been easier: the house more orderly, the will to work more simple and direct, relationships smoother, unity more natural, and the joy of living greater.

This is a fact!

And yet . . .

It did not take me long to learn that the first dreams fell to pieces once an imprudence was committed, and that a community collapsed once relationships between its elements became equivocal.

And the reason was always the same. Someone had sought to pluck a blossom from the flower-bed. Another had been hasty and insisted on tasting the bitter fruit. Above all, most men had given rein to their selfishness and turned love of woman into a hunting preserve.

Experience of mixed communities, of which the Church is the natural field, as also the parish, the movements, the groups, the liturgy itself, has shown me over and over again, that the problem is not a simple one, and has also explained, while not altogether justifying, the terror and anxiety influencing those people who cannot accept either co-educational schools, or mixed groups, or . . . you name it!

In some places, I remember, I have even seen naves of churches divided down the middle, with women on the left and men on the right. As if naves sufficed to separate material as explosive as that and designed to be together from dawn to dusk!

We still have a problem, it is clear – a big problem not to be underestimated, and in trying to solve it we must each recognize our own weaknesses and failures.

Even so, we must not turn back and rebuild the walls of separation we had in the past.

That would be impossible, and anachronistic as well.

We must go forward, even if it hurts, convinced that the times of a grown-up faith are upon us and that this problem not only has its negative aspects but extremely positive and valuable ones too.

I too have tried to go forward.

I have associated woman with my efforts to realize the Kingdom.

I have made a habit of reading the word of God with her.

I have tried to succour the poor and handicapped, by using her arms, which are more expert than mine.

I have given her my trust, and when she has given me her friendship, I have tried to concentrate my attention on her personality rather than on her body.

But what brought me to a final solution of the problem

was the deep-rooted, deeply experienced consideration that woman, all women, were not my brides but my sisters.

It may seem a small thing, but it was a big thing.

My love for my sisters helped me understand, and resolve within myself, love for woman, and to tame it without diminishing it.

I had never really understood the words of the Song of Songs, 'Oh, that you were my sister ... I could kiss you without people thinking ill of me.' (Cf. Song 8:1)

Now I understand, and I try to live that way.

Woman, all women, are my sisters.

I am no longer frightened by their bodies; their femininity leaves me serene.

No longer does their friendship disturb or weaken me.

I can even kiss them, if my kiss is brotherly, as Scripture says.

Yes, there is a kiss that shocks and there is a kiss that does not shock. And the kiss of a sister does not shock; it helps you live.

This is no light matter, of course, and I think all our striving for the Kingdom and our capacity for implementing God's command, 'You are to love your neighbour as yourself', have to be exercised here.

Yes, it is heroic.

But isn't everything Christ proposed heroic?

Isn't chastity heroic?

Isn't poverty heroic?

Aren't the Beatitudes heroic?

Isn't peace heroic?

And through this everyday heroism, nourished by grace and contemplation, we learn here below to become children of the Most High, and brothers and sisters of Jesus, who, when he came among us, did not separate men from women, but lived in simplicity with both, loved them all and scandalized no one.

Now, with your kind forbearance, let me tell you something else.

When I was a boy and I overheard girls sharing with one

another their daydream: 'Oh, how I wish I were a boy!' I used to feel a private complacency.

You're lucky, you're a man!

Now things are different . . . And for many, many reasons.

I am going to admit just one of them, one that comes from the heart.

I observe that women are better than I am.

Along the path to God, which is the one thing I care about, I always feel woman is a step or two ahead of me.

In humility humbler, in patience stronger, in charity more genuine.

I am not envious by nature. But it is easy to see that God looks with predilection on woman; more often than not, he says to me: Look and learn.

I would not want you to think I am trying to flatter women, or worse, that I am sentimentalizing over them.

I believe I am bearing witness to the truth and, more, to the personal virtue of every woman.

On the path to God, woman has special help.

Not for nothing are women more naturally religious. And this is not because they are weak.

It is because they are better made.

It is because God, when thinking about the creation, thought of it as being feminine.

How dear to God must be woman's 'abandonment' in love and in those things greater than she is.

What predilection he must have for her silence, open to the One who comes.

Not for nothing is Mary of Nazareth the greatest of all women and men, and the example for all.

5 Experience of God

Late have I loved thee, beauty so ancient and so new!
Late have I loved thee!
Thou wast within me, and I stood without.
I sought thee here, hurling my ugly self on
    the beauty of thy creatures.
Thou wast with me, but I was not with thee.
Thou hast called me, thy cry has vanquished my deafness.
Thou hast shone, and thy light has vanquished my
    blindness.
Thou hast broadcast thy perfume, and I have breathed
    it: now I sigh for thee.
I have tasted thee, and now I hunger for thee.
Thou hast touched me, and now I burn with desire for
    thy peace.   St Augustine

This is indeed a striking passage in the writings of the great
African mystic, and I must admit that it came to my help at
exactly the right moment.

When I first began to realize that I wanted to know God
by experience, I thought I had discovered a secret.

If God exists, I want to know him, I said in my heart.

Only knowledge can be of any help to me, since his mere
existing is not enough for me.

Indeed, Augustine himself had said 'Thou wast with me,
but I was not with thee.'

So there was a God . . . but still something was missing.

Yes, there was an I . . . there was a Thou . . . but this was
not sufficient.

I did not see him, I did not feel him.

Even if reason had brought me all the way to 'there is a Thou', what good would this do me if I did not make contact?

Something was missing, and I felt it in some anguish.

If God exists, I want to know him, I want to meet him.

'Thou hast called me, thy cry has vanquished my deafness. Thou hast shone, and thy light has vanquished my blindness. Thou hast broadcast thy perfume, and I have breathed it . . .'

Yes, the question was how to communicate.

The encounter had to be dynamic; static reason was no longer enough for me.

What a valuable intuition this was, coming to seed, as it did, in mid-life!

If God exists, I want to know him.

I want to meet him.

I want to grow accustomed to being near him.

I want to contemplate him.

It was no problem for me to abandon my accustomed quest for God by light of reason, which many people had recommended to me, and which, no doubt, had helped me at first.

But now this was no longer enough. Now I wanted to seek my God with my whole self and not merely with the proudest part of myself, my reason.

Meanwhile, I ought to say that the crisis had developed precisely there, in my reason; the culture of my times, even so-called Christian culture, no longer provided the security it had once provided.

It was hard to find a good professor of philosophy who could give sound advice. He was in crisis himself. I could feel it from a sort of sadness I saw in his eyes. Round me I detected a smell of worn-out things.

One had to go elsewhere, one had to get going, one had to attune one's ear to the 'voice', go down with Jacob to the ford of Jabbok (Genesis 32:23–32), where he had experienced God in an encounter which turned into a collision, and from which he emerged lame but enriched with something wonderfully new and important: 'the scent of God very near'.

One had to live, rather than reason. One had to be silent, rather than speak.

Life was much more explosive than mere reason. It had dimensions a great deal more universal.

There was no point in wasting time. I had to search, touch, listen, pray, love.

I remember when, during carnival time, my Catholic Action group assigned me to day-duty at the Turin Cottolengo hospital, caring for the sick and handicapped – people who are most visibly poor. And every evening I would leave transformed. Mankind, after that real, loving encounter in pain, seemed to me better, truer, realler.

And how can I ever forget the Easters I spent in the prisons, talking to the prisoners about the resurrection of Jesus!

How easy it became to weep with those who wept!

How visible the passage of peace where the Word had passed!

And what sweetness there was in mercy rediscovered by contact with the Absolute of God!

Christ had truly risen. This was no more a matter of words for me. It was life.

And what can I say about chastity as joy, about commitment as fulfilment, about forgiveness as peace, about toil as achievement, about service to one's fellow-man as the sweetness of living?

It was life that proved all that to me. And that was real life there: I saw it, I touched it, I experienced it.

Yes, today this is no longer a secret for me: human experience is already experience of God.

Our journey on earth is already a journey to heaven. Seeing a sunrise or a flower is already seeing God.

Discovering a galaxy with a telescope is a way of approaching your littleness to his greatness; basking in a sunny, flowering meadow is to glimpse the garment of the Eternal.

When I fall in love with something or someone, I feel God's call, and when I am eaten up with the insatiability inspired in me by some creature, I realize that God alone is the Absolute.

No, that it is no longer a secret; to seek to know God by experience, since all knowledge is experience of him.

Now, I understand that there is no other road, mysterious, often painful as it may be, and that we all have to take it, whether we want to or not.

He himself has marked it out.

Even sin leads me along his road, and perhaps leads me further than anything else.

For by fleeing from him, I have suffered from being without him, and by returning, I have come to know his heart better.

How true, the words attributed to St Teresa: 'If I could sin without offending anyone, I would, since I should learn to understand my God the better.'

But this is one of those mad ideas that true love thinks up.

One thing, however, is certain: once you have got there, evil cannot frighten you at all any more. You have won. You know that God is victor.

But unfortunately the victory is still not final.

Reason, once more, returns to the attack and undermines the position you have gained.

Yes, I admit: what made the acceptance of God as experience, as encounter, harder for me, was precisely reason – or rather, unloving reason, too-reasoning reason, reason unable to admit its own limitations and which, while still not having all available data, permits itself to say, at every new discovery: But this is impossible!

At bottom, this is the reasoning of someone who is not little of heart, of someone who would like to know everything all at once, of someone unable to put trust in someone greater than him and existing before him.

Not for nothing would Jesus tirelessly repeat his warning: '. . . unless you . . . become like little children you will never enter . . .' (Matthew 18:2). This is a threat we should all take to heart.

Well, I would never have thought pride was that dangerous and humility in one's relationship with God that needful.

In your pride, reason itself – God's great gift – ends up by being no more help to you. Indeed, it ultimately confounds you.

What a terrible thing reason is, for anyone who is not a little child, that is to say, for anyone bound up in himself, for anyone who does not seek, hence does not love, does not put his trust either in you or in God.

It is like a question obsessively repeated.

It is the inability to contemplate.

Basically it is the pride of one who believes only in self, thinks self to be the centre and basis of everything.

To reach certainty of God's existence, by experience, a person of this sort would need to have travelled the whole route, to have accumulated in his own brain or an electronic one all the data about God, with answers given to all the questions, and all the paradoxes and contradictions reconciled.

Is this possible?

No, it is not possible.

Hence it is said that 'God resists the proud', and that is no joke.

Like it or not, life is a road, and reason too is one of the travellers.

And on the road, you have to learn how to wait. You have to experience your poverty, you have to accept the dark night, or the fog unexpectedly rising and on occasion blotting out the sun.

But while you are waiting . . .

While you are in the darkness . . .

While you are humbly asking your reason to take a few minutes off, to close its eyes and take a little nap, if only from exhaustion, try and see if there are any other potentialities in you, which may be able to help you over your incessant doubts.

Try to let yourself go, on the arid sand of your desert, as you follow your track through it.

Who knows, you may find something else that can be helpful.

Try it!

I have tried it!

And this is what the contemplative Psalm tells you:

Yahweh, my heart has no lofty ambitions, my eyes are not
   raised too high;
I am not concerned with great affairs or marvels beyond
   my scope.
Enough for me to keep my soul tranquil and quiet like a
   child in its mother's arms;
as content as a child that has been weaned.

(Psalm 131:1–2).

Weary of reasoning, I tried to love.

I thought of myself as a babe in God's arms, as if they had
been my mother's.

And so I fell asleep.

Then contemplation came to me.

And contemplation is loving.

Contemplation is beyond meditation, even the highest and
deepest meditation.

In contemplation I had experience of God.

As doubt lurked in reason, so in contemplation doubt
vanished.

I experienced that God gives himself to those who abandon
themselves totally.

And in his self-giving and your self-giving, you no longer
reason.

True love is madness, God's madness, the creature's
madness.

In this madness, you contemplate.

O the fiery nights of his embrace!

O the fullness of giving!

O the transcendence of all things visible!

O the love that conquers all!

What is all else in comparison with this?

'A straw', said Thomas.

'Nothing', said John of the Cross.

Brothers and sisters, would you like a piece of advice?

Don't waste any more time wondering if God exists.

The Real One will see to telling you that, in every possible
way. All existence will repeat it to you.

And if you do not see him, this only means that you are blind. And if you do not hear him, it means you must be deaf.

Strive no more, it is a vain task.

Try to touch him, and you can touch him in love.

Love, and all becomes logical, easy and true.

You can touch him directly, in nights of contemplation, when he unveils himself to your loving passivity.

You can touch him indirectly, by serving his creatures, in sincere, open-hearted service.

But love!

The problem of God is a problem of communication.

And communication is called Holy Spirit.

We shall discover God by encounter, but inside not outside ourselves.

Inside not outside him.

Indeed, Jesus says, at the peak of his joy, encountering the Father: You in me and I in you, so that we may be perfect in unity (cf. John 17:21–2).

And to us, too, he gives the same opportunity, promising us the Spirit. And to convince us, he states a truth which is perhaps the greatest experience we can have of him: 'On that day you will have no further questions to ask me' (John 16:23).

I would never have thought that a moment like that could exist in life: a moment so luminous that you no longer feel like asking questions. 'On that day you will have no further questions to ask me.'

There is no further need.

At that moment, everything is so clear that all you can say is: Enough!

Everything is so joyous that all you can say to him is: Thank you!

Yes, all is One, all is Three.

They say the mystery of the Trinity is incomprehensible, and they may be right!

But it is so simple when you live in it!

Nothing is more luminous and true when you experience it.

What would the Father be without Jesus?

And what would Jesus be without the Father?

And where would fullness of joy be without the Spirit uniting them, making these three one?

Have you ever tried thinking of Jesus' cry in the darkness, his prayer in the desert or in Gethsemane?

Had the Father not been there to answer him, what would have become of him, or us?

What loneliness – that of a God alone in his fearsome oneness!

No, Jesus cried out and the Father answered him and Love is what eternally unites them.

What joy, the Spirit!

He makes the three one, and in that restored unity resides the bliss of God!

All is One, all is Three.

In unity we begin, but it is in the Trinity that we grasp God's fullness.

Perfection is in the Trinity.

I, Thou, Love.

The Father, the Son, the Spirit.

The Spirit is the embrace that makes you three Persons one, and gives you the joy of being one.

The Kingdom is the unity in the multiplicity of all, it is the bliss of being a single thing, and the joy of paradise.

When, in the desert, I experienced the mystery of the love of God as Trinity, I threw myself down on the sand and rolled about with joy, shouting 'I love you too!' and I felt full.

In his grasp, a living communication, I understood the relativity of all things and the absolute of our sharing in the divine life, that is to say, God's everlasting love.

And reason? Where had reason taken itself?

Reason, ever ready to make indiscreet inquiries, where had it hidden while I was contemplating?

It was on its knees, nearby on the arid sand, reduced at last to silence, thunderstruck as I.

Like a little girl.

Little, as love would have her.

And I said in my ecstasy: Thank you, my God!

Thank you.

6 What Does *Not* Exist: Chance

It has taken me some time, but now I've got it.

And very pleased I am.

And I want to pass it on to the little ones, the littlest ones among you, my friends. I want to pass it on to you as a simple but very, very important secret: as one of those truths you arrive at after much journeying, after much thinking, and making everything clear to you in one or two words but enough to solve huge problems which have bothered you all your life and round which you have vainly twisted and turned, wearing yourself out and complicating the simplest things *ad infinitum*.

This is the secret. *Chance does not exist.*

Chance is a word without meaning, and even though it recurs *ad infinitum* in our manner of thinking and acting, it is a mere phantom, the erroneous solution to a problem, something accepted by the truly ignorant or, rather, blind.

Chance does not exist.

Unless by 'chance' we mean what Anatole France says so well with this striking aphorism: 'Chance is the pseudonym God uses when he does not choose to sign his name.'

No, *chance does not exist.*

The only thing that exists is God's will; a will that fills the entire universe, steers the stars, sets the seasons, calls all things by name, gives life and gives death, provides for the creatures, clothes them in beauty and harmony – and especially, wills the salvation of all, vanquishes evil, builds his kingdom, which is a kingdom of justice and peace, a kingdom of truth and love, a kingdom of resurrection and life.

Nothing escapes this will.

Not a cell is out of place. Not an atom is there by chance. Not a number fails to count in the totality of the universe.

History, the manifestation of this ineffable, mighty, often hidden, incomprehensible and painful labour, is perfectly dominated by this will, which leads it towards the blazing manifestation of the children of God.

Evil, darkness, suffering, physical death are only the necessary stages along the highroad we are all travelling, to make God's victory more true, more luminous, more total and more obvious.

From now on, I shall never attribute things to chance. I shall say prayerfully: This is your will, O Lord.

I have always loved the story of Jesus' first meeting with Nathanael, as John describes it in the first chapter of his Gospel.

'What a coincidence!' I would once have said. But now I would not say that any more.

Here is the passage, in all its vividness:

The next day, after Jesus had decided to leave for Galilee, he met Philip and said, 'Follow me'. Philip came from the same town, Bethsaida, as Andrew and Peter. Philip found Nathanael and said to him, 'We have found the one Moses wrote about in the Law, the one about whom the prophets wrote: he is Jesus son of Joseph, from Nazareth'. 'From Nazareth?' said Nathanael. 'Can anything good come from that place?' 'Come and see', replied Philip.

When Jesus saw Nathanael coming he said to him, 'There is an Israelite who deserves the name, incapable of deceit'. 'How do you know me?' said Nathanael. 'Before Philip came to call you,' said Jesus 'I saw you under the fig tree.' Nathanael answered, 'Rabbi, you are the Son of God, you are the King of Israel'. Jesus replied, 'You believe that just because I said: I saw you under the fig tree. You will see greater things than that.' (John 1:43–50)

And you, how did your first meeting with God occur?

Was it like Nathanael's? If so, this means you must be very simple and possess that same celebrated childlikeness of spirit as Nathanael possessed and was praised for by Jesus himself: allowing you not to attribute the meeting to chance any longer, but to something quite precise and quite clear.

Can you believe he saw you under the fig tree?

And not only under the fig tree.

Can you believe he thought of you and looked for you before you thought of him and became aware of his presence in your life?

Of course, it takes a little while to convince ourselves of the simplicity of the things of God.

We shall go on wondering: 'Is that possible?'

Yes, he seems to have guessed right . . . but . . . maybe it is just a coincidence.

Yes, he saw me under the fig tree, but will he see me in the woodshed? And will he still see me in the fog? And when he is distracted, will he remember me then?

When I lie on my bed of pain will he be present, watching me?

And if I'm out of work, why doesn't he do something?

Does he really know I want a husband?

Why doesn't he answer, when I'm living in mortal terror of being alone all my life?

The road is long as we walk round and round this mysterious sanctuary of ours, the sanctuary of our complexities and doubts.

It takes time to acquire the straightforwardness of a Nathanael and joyfully cry: 'You are the Son of God!'

You are no accident!

You are a will, seeking me and seeing me!

You are . . . Person!

If only I could really believe!

What if I really could?

What if I decided to think that chance does not exist?

What if I tried to live with a God ever present in my affairs, even the most trivial?

Friends, the answer that emerges is wondrous, wondrous, wondrous!

Have you ever tried it?

Here is something that will make some of you smile, but as long as we are on the subject of testimony, I want to tell you about something that happened to me – something I experienced and still experience intensely.

I tried it and I succeeded.

And the fact has had no small effect on my relationship with God.

Listen.

Exactly twenty years ago, my Prior, Father Voillaume, gave me the assignment of founding a community of Little Brothers at Marseilles, to accommodate brothers returning from the foreign missions, if they needed somewhere quiet in the country.

There was not much choice, but I was lucky enough to find a little farm on the outskirts of the city, where brothers ailing or healthy could help to balance the community's budget – with its eleven cows, seven pairs of pigeons and a hundred or so chickens.

We sold milk, cheese and eggs to our neighbours in the district.

The only brother there was, a really fine fellow who knew all about looking after livestock, was a young Fleming with a great will to work, and he kept the business on its feet. Only, once he fell asleep, he could not wake up.

I had a first-class alarm clock, the kind especially made for hard cases, and I must say I loved it dearly. Every evening I had to lend it to Ulrich, and he was very keen on it too.

Here begins the story of the God who wakes me up under a fig tree.

One evening I told Ulrich: 'Here's the clock. I'm giving it to you to keep. I'll get the Lord to wake me up.'

Ulrich looked at me with a beautiful smile, like the smile of God testing my faith.

Will you believe what happened?

Twenty years passed . . . Multiply 20 by 365 days, and throw in the leap years, and you get a pretty big number!

The alarm clock I opted for that night, in faith, has always worked to perfection, and ever since I have forbidden myself any mechanical interference with my ears, such as that of the alarm clock I gave away to Ulrich that evening but, deep down, really wanted for the sake of yet another security in life.

Now I wager my security at risk of my faith and rely on being awakened by God.

Faith is all that is needed to assure the functioning of the invisible alarm clock of his presence in my life.

I grant, it is not always easy. In fact it is a matter demanding my unremitting commitment. But I do not mind telling you that my day begins with the joy of repeating with Isaiah, 'Each morning he wakes me to hear, to listen like a disciple' (Isaiah 50:4).

What a wondrous thing!

And so simple!

It is enough to believe. It is enough to depend on him, it is enough to rely on his ever-present presence.

As God sees Nathanael under the fig tree, so he sees me too, and calls me, because my faith calls to him.

And it is always a great occasion of joy for me to reflect that he has seen me, has thought of me and, as if that were not enough, that he says to me: 'Does this surprise you? You will see greater things than that' (cf. John 1:50).

Summing up, then . . .

As I have told you, you sense God at the outset of your journey in the sign of the creation.

Then, reason helps you reflect on this and discover a certain logic in it, as you strive to assign meaning to the real world around you.

Then, you put reason aside, because it gets you in a muddle owing to its limitations, and its proud insistence on showing how smart it is.

Then love steps in, great love, and just when you are no longer able to meditate, you find yourself asleep in Love's arms.

This is contemplation, the true revelation of God: *the personal, savoury, dark, passive, often painful revelation of him,* as Maritain says in his *God and the Ways of Knowing.*

When you love, really love, everything becomes easier, and you realize you have found.

Yes, I found because I loved.

And I found because I let myself go, in the darkness.

But the darkness is light for him and he can touch me when he wishes, and there is no longer a veil between his and my loving nakedness.

A fantastic thing, love!

And it asks me one thing only: to give him more, to give him all.

And what is the most precious thing in me that I can give him?

Which is the gift he most loves?

Trust.

Of all the gifts you can give a person, the greatest is trust.

I trust you.

I feel you are with me.

And with you I am at peace.

You know, you are able, you provide!

This is pure faith, naked faith. This is the faith of one who knows how to love.

And so, can you wonder, when Francis wants to know God's will, that he opens the Bible at random – 'by chance'?

Are you surprised when the newborn Church, faced with choosing a replacement for Judas, who has turned traitor, draws lots?

Was it childish to open the Bible at random?

Was it childish to draw lots over an important choice?

Of course it was childish. But these were children that felt themselves safe in the arms of the Father, in the arms of someone who would not deceive them, in the arms of a will that I seek in love, and which cannot play tricks on me.

When I am at this point, I sense that God is not playing tricks on me but answering me accurately and kindly.

Many times I have re-read, in the *Little Flowers* of Saint Francis, the story of how Francis and Masseo were walking along a road in Tuscany. Masseo was a little in the lead, with Francis following him in silence.

Masseo said, 'Brother Francis, here are two roads in front of me. Which one shall we take?'

'Whichever one the Lord wishes,' replied Francis.

'But how shall I know which one the Lord wishes?' objected Masseo. 'There are two of them.'

'This is how he will show us. Stand at the fork and turn round and round, as children do at play.' And Brother Masseo began spinning like a top, until he fell dazed to the ground.

'Which do you see before you,' Francis asked him, 'the road to Arezzo or the one to Sienna?'

'I see the road to Sienna.'

'Very well, we shall go to Sienna,' Francis concluded, not yet knowing that, in Sienna, rival factions were at each other's throats, and that God had indicated this city to him precisely so that he might bring his peace there, which indeed he did.

You may laugh, if you think yourself an intellectual, but if you have the heart of a child perhaps you may discover a secret that will help you in life.

I know that many people do not proceed in this way. I know that the clever ones would be ashamed to do so.

Anyhow, we are not all bound to act in the same way. We each have our own path to follow, and each does well to follow it according to his lights.

This is what I do, and the testimony I can offer you is that, yes, I have felt God present in the cosmos, yes, I have felt him in history, yes, I have felt him in the Church; but I have felt him much more present in the intimacy I have tried to achieve with him in little things, in the things of every day.

Yes, brothers and sisters, that is all I have to say.

Intimacy with God is the highest form of experience that I have had with him.

Intimacy with God has ever been the clearest answer as to whether he exists and whether he is present in my life.

7 'I Living in Them, You Living in Me – That Their Unity May Be Complete'

Now that I have reached the end of my journey of knowing God by experience on earth, I feel that there could be no more exact way of summing up one's relationship with him as the Transcendent, the Absolute, the Wonderful, the Merciful, than the words John reports from the Last Supper – Jesus' words in his last farewell to his own:

> With me in them and you in me, may they be so completely one that the world will realise that it was you who sent me ... (John 17:23)

I have repeatedly said in this book that modern atheism tends to beg the question, owing in most cases to the difficulty of accepting a portrait of God, initially deformed by our juvenile religious concepts and then repeatedly erased by our maturing reason, as reason veers this way and that under varying cultural impacts. For reason alters in function of personal experience.

Let me put it yet another way. In childhood, the notion of God comes to us as the colossal, the 'immense', the measure-less, associated with everything large, as something infinitely surpassing us. God is the One who can do whatever we cannot. He is the Creator, the Almighty, the Strong One, the All-Knowing One. And we? We are the small ones, 'unable' ones, weak ones, sinners.

In a word, God is All, we are Nothing.

And this is true!

But it is true ... well, only relatively true. It is truth on its way to being 'truer and truer', on its way towards a truth needing explanation and needing to explain. And when this truth is fully arrived at, it looks very different from the original intuition.

This is where the problem lies, or rather, the obstacle, sooner or later creating difficulties and making the truth arrived at in childhood seem irrational.

What contact can I possibly have with a God so fine, so happy, so high, when I am so wretched, so distressed, so everlastingly defeated?

Initially I cannot do without him. In my fear or immaturity, aggravated by the notion of eternal punishment, which adults are all to ready to instil in me, I cannot do without him. But there comes a moment when I react against this, usually in an unruly, mixed-up way.

Then my life grows full of compromises, of peaks and troughs; in fear I stand guilty before God. But my relationship with him is becoming weaker now, entangled in a new jungle of faith and non-faith, sin and guilt-complexes, night-fears, and the constant bad example I eventually give my brothers, my sisters and myself.

And here I suddenly see, with a start, that my religious paraphernalia is more superstition than theology, more darkness than light, more clammy, uncomfortable fog than radiant sunshine, more . . . yes, more practical atheism than liberating hope.

Where have I gone wrong?

The error at the basis of my whole conception of God, is: *separation*.

God is up there and I am down here. And separated from him by hundreds of millions of light years into the bargain.

The tragic part of the error lies in the name I use for the place where he dwells, the sphere where he lives, the house where he dwells, the name we repeat so casually, the beautiful name, 'heaven'.

When I was a lad, 'heaven' for me meant 'away up there', the place beyond the stars, the brilliant azure blanket over the earth, and it was easy for me to imagine the soul of my departed grandmother, back in those days, flying up to 'heaven', diaphanous as air, far, far into the distance – to a place we living persons could not reach, weighed down as we were by a sinful body that could not fly.

It seems comical now. But do you realize, without the word of God, without theology, this sort of conceptual thinking can lead straight to atheism? Or if not actually to atheism, to religious indifferentism? The least that can happen is that you learn to go it alone and come to believe in the terrible possibility lurking in the title of one of A. J. Cronin's best novels: *The Stars Look Down.*

Yes, heaven stops looking down at you. God stops looking down at you. And you end by believing that God is perfectly indifferent to you, especially when you are in trouble.

I do not know what your experience has been, but I know what happened to me and I can assure you it took a long time to get things straight again and give the word 'heaven' its correct, or at least a plausible, location.

We have to grasp that the culture in which we are steeped, the so-called 'current view of religion' with which the media bombard us, especially here in the West, is completely devoid of theological content and even more devoid of experience of God.

At very best we are purveyed a load of superstitions, trite, worn-out commonplaces, absolutely alien to the great, single, sublime mystery of the Unity in Trinity of God, which is the epitome of all visible and invisible reality, the answer to all the problems, the environment in which we live like fish in water or birds in air, the teeming womb of Love.

Heaven is not up there – though it is up there too.

Heaven is everywhere.

Heaven is up there and down here.

Heaven is the infinitely far and the infinitely near.

Heaven is the secret place, that is, the hidden place, where my Creator lives, and where I, his creature live, where he is there as Father and I am there as child, where he is the spring, and I am the one who thirsts, where he creates and inspires, and I have the potential to create and inspire.

Heaven is everywhere, because God is everywhere; and it is called heaven because God is mystery, he is hidden. And it is right that his dwelling-place should be called this, out of deference to my immaturity in my 'becoming', out of deference to my inclination to half-close my eyes on the path towards the fullness of the All, the path of my progressive discovery of God as Person.

And because this is so, the light has need of darkness, life must touch non-life, selfless love must discover the fact of selfishness, truth must make its way through the lie, virtue must do battle with sin.

Yes, it is true, I discover the positive of God in the negative of me and the universe, and I know that you need both to have a beautiful photograph.

This is experience of God.

God becomes man so that man may become God, sorrow become joy, the Nothing become the All.

It is meeting.

It is togetherness.

It is begetting.

It is the maturing of the child in the Father's shadow.

It is the Kingdom of love.

It is the everlasting.

It is paradise.

You living in me and I living in you. Behold, journey's end.

When I was a boy I looked for God by directing my gaze towards the light coming from on high.

As a lad I looked for him in my brothers and sisters around me.

When I grew up I sought him along desert tracks.

Now I have come to the end of the road, I have only to close my eyes and there he is, within me.

If I see light I see him in the light, and if I see darkness I feel him in the darkness. But always within me.

I no longer even feel the need to search for him, or to kneel down to pray, or to think or speak in order to communicate with him.

I only need to think of my human state – and there, in faith, I see him in the midst.

You living in me and I living in you, I say with John. And John it is, the great Gospel mystic, who records yet another of

Jesus' sayings, surely the most concise of all the syntheses of contemplation and action, of heaven and earth, of doing and being: *Live on in my love* (cf. John 15:9).

Live on . . . live on . . .

I want to conclude with a few words about this 'Live on in my love', which John reports as addressed by Jesus to each of us.

This 'Live on' is a stringent command, much more binding than a pious exhortation.

Anyone who comes to realize what this 'Live on' means, has completed the cycle of the quest, has closed the circle of experience of God and no longer needs to wonder where God is or how to make living contact with him.

You living in me and I living in you. The creature's long pilgrimage is over.

Now Pilgrim abides in an eternal embrace, in a boundless relationship, in certitude ever more certain.

You living in me and I living in you, we repeat, as Jesus repeated on the night of love, when self-giving grows into the implacable demand of the creature caught up in its Creator's embrace.

You living in me and I living in you, cries Pilgrim who has come from very far away and has so long sought the One who was quite near although unseen, as Augustine recounts in his *Confessions*.

You living in me and I living in you, sighs the creature who thought to be satisfied with idols and the void, and now discovers that God alone is the Absolute, here, close, true, unique, accessible.

But more. I notice, in this 'I living in you', the true metaphysical face of the divine–human relationship.

Let me try to explain what I mean.

Most of those who set off in search of God stop halfway there, because God is silent. They try shouting, and he does not answer.

Not a sound.

Every day someone questions me about this 'silence' on God's part.

'I speak, I call, I beg, and he doesn't answer me.' And the silence is interpreted as absence.

God does not answer me.

So there is no God.

How long it takes to grasp this fact, to understand about the way God acts!

What lengths we go to, trying to breach this silence! Our eyes are directed towards the Invisible, in hopes of finally seeing something.

My eyes strain till they hurt, trying to glimpse something that will speak to me, something that will tell me it is there, something that will be the start of a dialogue with me.

And I see nothing.

My ears hear nothing.

And I withdraw, disillusioned, and begin to doubt my faith.

I have not yet come to understand that it is well things are the way they are, and that this not-seeing-with-my-eyes and not-hearing-with-my-ears is a sign that I am still in control of my nerves, and far from the quicksand of superstition and hallucination.

Now that I am an expert on all this – especially on God's silence – and someone comes to me and tells me of having seen . . . a light . . . of having heard . . . a voice . . . of noticing a spring of water . . . I tell that person in no uncertain terms, 'Friend, you ought to go to a psychiatrist. You're on the edge of mental illness.'

No: just as the visible is not the invisible, just as nature is not grace, so our alphabet is not God's alphabet, our language is not his language, our ears are not his ears.

When God speaks, no vocal cords vibrate – and the place where you are 'hearing' these voices is certainly not in your ear.

If he wishes to say something to me – and he is continually telling me things, since God is Word – he tells me in the most hidden and mysterious part of my being, the place we sometimes call our heart and sometimes our conscience.

It is not easy to know where this place is, this locus of encounter, this marvel of our being.

We know there is such a place. We have continuous experience of it and we perceive the voices that speak there even if we have been born deaf.

God speaks with the Reality that is himself, and speaks to the reality that I am.

He speaks in the language of reality.

What happens is what happens with the stars.

When one star wishes to speak to another, it does not use a mouth, since it does not have one, nor ears, which it does not possess, and which would be useless to it – but speaks through the law of gravity, which it does possess, through the law of the attraction of bodies, in and by which it lives.

And it can say: You are near me, sister star, by your radiance, and far from me by your distance, where Reality has placed you.

God speaks to the human being through reality and, apart from this reality, his speech is absolute silence. God, who is Word, has very reality for his language, and this is where we should listen for him.

And it is an ongoing discourse, an endless, inexhaustible love-song, a harmony that never dies away, a dialogue that never flags, a computer always turned on.

Yes, God speaks through the things that are, through the logic that rules them, through the ends towards which they make their way.

God does not tell me with his lips that he is beauty, he shows me this beauty in sunset or in the sparkling of the ocean.

He does not tell me he is everlasting, he astounds me day by day with the dawn.

He does not tell me he is life and fertility, he gives me a field of rich, ripe grain.

He does not tell me I must die, he makes me die.

He does not tell me I shall rise again, he shows me that Christ is risen.

He does not tell me that he thinks about me and loves me, he puts charity in my heart, which is his way of loving.

He does not tell me what I ought to do, he draws this out of my own conscience, where he everlastingly abides.

And the Bible – the written word of God, as we say – what is the Bible?

I shall tell you what it is. It is just what I have been saying.

It is the Reality of God speaking to the reality of me. It is truly *You living in me and I living in you*, that we may be perfectly united.

Do you really believe that, when the sacred authors were writing the books of the Bible, they heard the Word of God in their ears?

Do you think that the Evangelists had their tape recorders going on the desk beside them?

Or that the prophets wrote their burning words passively, like robots?

Here lies the real mystery of the relationship between God and man – the unfathomable secret of the place of encounter, the impossibility of distinguishing between what he does and what the little child does who is within him, between what he says and what the hand of the child living within him puts on paper.

When Ezekiel sees water gushing from the right side of the Temple, growing deeper and deeper, mounting to his calves, then to his waist, then swelling to the proportions of a navigable river, do you really think that the stones of the Temple were actually awash in water?

No, do not be so childish when considering the truth of the sacred words.

There was God, in the Temple, and there was Ezekiel, and the Word becomes word in that very encounter. The vision is a sign of what God wishes to say to those who are ready to grasp it.

You living in me and I living in you. You speak and I write, and at a certain point the two realities become one.

If you were to fall silent, I should speak myself, for, by virtue of being within you, I become you.

You have told me 'not to kill', and I have written that down. Now, even if you stop telling me this, I shall keep on writing it because, in becoming your will, I myself understand that one ought not to kill.

It is no accident that the more mature books of the Bible were written at least twice over, and the most beautiful passages were mulled over again after the Babylonian captivity, all the way back to Genesis.

It was still the same Word, but the echo in the heart of God's child had become clearer and deeper.

Everything is on the move, everything is becoming. Even the Word is on the move, a mutual experiment, a ripening, a maturing, a heading towards that extraordinary phenomenon experienced as *You living in me and I living in you*.

And this You is God himself – and I, living in him, become himself, living in his Son.

You!
   I!
What should I be without you?
But what would you be without me?
What would Jesus be without the Father?
And really . . . can you imagine the Father without Jesus?
The mystical Reality is the Relationship, and the Relationship is called the Holy Spirit.
'My Father goes on working, and so do I' (John 5:17).
There are not two mysteries: God, and man.
There is only one, and both are one, and always found together.

I cannot disconnect myself from my God. He is the being of my being, the root of my root, and all things converge on the unity of Being.

And hence, a woman's womb with a child in it is the best simile we have for the relationship between God and man, the sign best symbolizing that reality.

No longer seek God far away from you. Seek him within yourself, and abide in his presence.
'Let yourself go. Let God act.'
But your letting go must be perpetual activity, like a road

unmoving yet leading on to somewhere, like a yes pronounced in concert, deliberately, for ever.

God is what you seek as perfection, as being, as oneness, as love.

God is on the point of your pencil, on the edge of your ploughshare, as Teilhard de Chardin said.

The only thing separating you from God is the placenta of his procreative force, his infinite respect for your individuality, space in which you can be free to say 'I love you', distance allowing him to embrace you as son or daughter, brother, friend, spouse . . . an autonomous person.

I sought – yes, I sought, for he was seeking me. That is my answer. I found him because he was already there, waiting for me.

Part Two

EXPERIENCE OF THE CHURCH

On this earth, experience of God invariably involves us, sooner or later, in experience of the Church.

The two tensions – the one, towards God and the other towards one's fellow-man – are linked to the mystery of the cross, being symbolized respectively by its vertical stock and horizontal arms.

It was not otherwise for me; my progressive entry into the mystery of God has been accompanied by the discovery of the mystery of Church.

In the second part of this book, I touch on some of the problems which arise from this double tension, and which, in my estimation, are of a relevance I make no bones about calling prophetic for the Church of today.

8   Getting Married – a Defect?

Yes, I must admit, I have had a happy life; and now that I am at the end of the race, I can tell you I know what I'm talking about.

Three gifts of God have been at the root of my joy, and have lighted my road:

1   A family poor and at peace.
2   A community of faith and prayer, for example Catholic Action Youth, leading me to more intimate knowledge of Christ and giving me a taste for church life.
3   A call to the desert and the contemplative life.

I have tried to live these three stages at full intensity, and they have never let me down. If I had to live my life all over again, I would live each of those stages again, in full awareness of what I was doing.

Certainly, the call to the desert, though the hardest, has been the most uplifting of them,

the most beautiful,

the most mature,

the freest.

The desert is soul-space. It is faith lived without frontiers. It is the alcove of delights for the meeting with the Spirit. It is – and this cannot be questioned – what precedes the Promised Land.

In the desert I experienced the real ordeals of faith, the dark night, but I also experienced the dazzling victory of God over human nature.

I experienced the temptations of the idols hidden under the camel-saddle, as Rachel did when fleeing from her father's house with Jacob (Genesis 31:34). But this was precisely when I began to savour, in those glittering nights, the primacy of the Beatitudes pronounced by Christ, that pinnacle of human experience on earth.

'How happy are the poor in spirit . . .

'Happy those who hunger and thirst for what is right . . .

'Happy the merciful . . .

'Happy the peacemakers . . .' (Matthew 5:3 ff.).

But these gifts of prayer, these gifts of self-offering, these gifts of the Beatitudes, are available to everybody.

Absolutely everybody.

And yet how many times I have heard people say:

'Lucky you . . .

'It's all very well for you . . . you aren't married . . .

'Marriage is a very different matter!

'When you have a family, everything's different . . .

'If I'd got married, I'd feel as though I had lost something, had dampened my enthusiasm . . . had diminished my charity.'

This 'celibate mentality' is still very current in the Church today, the notion that the total accomplishment of Christianity is only possible if you give up marriage!

This is a difficult taboo to root out, and many churchmen, and churchwomen even more so, often give the impression that they believe it and do not want to be completely freed from these inaccurate conceptions about life.

To be sure, there are many vocations, and we each have our own.

To be sure, there is such a thing as the call to virginity, especially following Jesus' example. But it is just as sure that there is the vocation to marriage, and it is not weak or slothful to embrace it, especially today.

I do not want to offend anyone by saying this, but the Church, particularly in recent centuries, has presided over a certain devaluation of the married state. A clerical mentality has spread abroad, concentrating on, preaching and exalting, celibacy alone, and thus implanting in the Christian subconscious the idea that when people marry they become second-class Christians, unsuited to leading a prayer community and unworthy of touching sacred things.

Now perhaps the time has come . . .

Pope John Paul, whom many people regard as a traditionalist, is the very pontiff to have had the guts to go against the stream and, faced with this celibate mentality, make declarations clearer than any other pope in recent centuries.

Speaking to married couples in St Peter's Square, he said:

> Marriage is not inferior to celibacy, and Christian perfection is measured by the yardstick of charity, not the one of continence . . .
>
> Christ's words afford no pretext for maintaining either the inferiority of marriage or the superiority of virginity and celibacy.
>
> Marriage and continence are not mutually opposed, nor do they separate the human and Christian community into two camps, as it were – that of the perfect, by reason of their continence, and that of the 'imperfect', or less perfect, by virtue of their conjugal life.
>
> There is no basis for the antithetical notion that celibate or unmarried persons, merely by virtue of continence, constitute the class of the perfect, and contrariwise that married persons constitute that of the non-perfect or less perfect.

For me to believe the Pope's courageous statement as absolutely true, I only have to call to mind my own father and mother. Four of us children entered religion. But not one of us, seriously committed to our vocations as we were, has been able to dream of equalling my mother's charity, or my father's simple, heroic faith.

What about that?

Listen to this story. I lived in the desert in middle life, when real experience pulls you out of all fumes of superstition and teaches you to make realistic judgements about things and people.

When I was in the desert I earned my daily bread as a meteorologist.

My work consisted in visiting five stations I had set up, which recorded data on temperature, humidity, wind direction and velocity, rainfall – things like that.

It was interesting work, and it earned me the wherewithal to travel the desert trails, where I found Tuareg encampments, work camps, uranium and diamond prospectors, and, most valued of all, wells of sweet water.

For some time I had been in contact with a Swedish engineer, who had been converted to Catholicism, and whom I had been meeting and instructing for about two years. Now he wanted me to baptize him, on his work site, among his colleagues, in a work camp of prospectors for precious minerals, between Ideles and Djanèt.

On my way through Laghouat, the centre of the diocese, I asked and received the bishop's permission to do this, and, in high heart, fixed the date for the ceremony which Alex, the neophyte, wanted.

The stage seemed set for a magnificent demonstration of faith, in that lost region of the Sahara.

On the date agreed, as though drawn there by grace and friendship, geographers, prospectors, doctors, from camps hundreds of kilometres away all round, agreed to meet in this wild, lonely place in the desert called Tabelbellà.

I arrived two days before the christening. And it was well that I did, for there was a big surprise waiting for me.

As well as the tents of the prospectors' camp, I found a big tent pitched by the regional health service.

In it, a young married couple, both doctors, had set up shop, and I found them hard at work treating the sick of the area. Many people had come, from far away, and these formed a long queue waiting to be examined by the *toubib*.

The couple were Belgians, who had got married and then set out for Africa. They had taken on the extremely hard work of going out and finding the sick in the nomad encampments, and their life was certainly not a 'middle-class', comfortable one.

But they were magnificent. I was moved, to watch them at work.

I remember them as if it were today.

Young and courageous, they bent attentively over their patients as these filed past one by one, trusting and grateful.

All wanted to take them back to their various encampments for supper, promising *couscous* or *michouy*, their eyes sparkling with joy and gratitude.

I felt uplifted, watching these young doctors and wished they could have been on all the European and American television screens, to demonstrate by their actions that there is no unemployment in the world for people who live in charity and seek communion with the poor.

Just as there was no unemployment for those who spent their lives out there looking for water, to treat it and channel it for the thirsty population, or building villages in an attempt to make the life of the poor more humane.

Inside the tent where we gathered next evening for Alex's baptism, there was as interesting a congregation as ever I could wish to see.

What surprised me was that we were all practising Christians, and that nearly all had been members of militant movements such as the Young Christian Workers, the Belgian Student Youth, the Focolare, the Neo-Catechumenal Way communities, and family spirituality movements.

The Holy Spirit descended on us, gathered there as the Church, and when I poured the water over Alex's head there was general emotion and the joy of all was plain to see.

Then we sat down and each in turn spoke of his or her pilgrimage in the faith.

I was impressed by the maturity of these people, who had gone out there to work, certainly, but most of all for an ideal they had acquired.

Here are their testimonies as I remember them.

Jean and Yvette: We are French. We were active together in the Young Christian Workers. We fell in love, got married, and came out here with a team of uranium prospectors.

I pilot the helicopter, and Yvette is camp secretary. We're very happy and mean to stay in Africa as long as we can.

We have many, many friends among the Arabs and Berbers, and we help them in every way we can.

We're happy to be here, and to have borne witness to Christ before our brother Alex, who has received baptism today.

Monique and Pierre: We are Belgians, doctors. We come from Student Youth, but we met in an early Mariapolis of the Focolare. Everything changed after that. Jesus 'took us over'. When we are with our fellow-Christians, we feel that he too is with us, and this is our strength, our deep inspiration.

We want to work as doctors in the Third World.

We enjoy our work, we're fond of each other, and from now on we're going to think of life as a gift offered to God and our fellow-men.

We've got used to the desert. In fact, we've fallen in love with it. And we're happy to be here this evening to testify to our love for Christ, who has called Alex to follow him today.

Francesco and Clara: We're Italians. I'm an engineer [Francesco]. I met Clara on a Neo-Catechumenal catechetics weekend. We're treading the path of faith together, and this helps our married life a lot. We're happy to be here to tell Alex of our affection.

Alex: I come from very far away. My father had a steelworks in Stockholm and wanted me to work with him. I had an identity crisis. I was on bad terms with myself, I could find nothing to live for and drifted about all over the world.

I've been to every continent and known many people who, like me, were looking for something. In India I got on to drugs and just about went over the brink.

A woman who loved me saved me, and later I married her.

Then all of a sudden I was alone again. She died of cancer, in an American hospital.

I was in despair. Off I went again, with her memory as my sole support. She was a believing and practising Christian, and on her deathbed she'd left me her little wooden crucifix, saying, 'This will save you.'

Just to go on living, I threw myself into my work. I had

taken employment with a mining company working here in
Algeria.

One day out on the road I met Brother Carlo.

From then on I felt that the moment had come to listen to
what Susie had told me – Susie was my wife who died. I
always feel her near me. She is my inspiration.

I asked to be baptized.

Now here I am with you, and full of joy to be here.

I'm not alone any more, since I've found a Church.

I feel as though my life were just beginning.

When everyone had finished telling the story of their lives,
there was a moment of silence in the tent. The Spirit's fire
had welded us into a unity. Emotion was strong and visible.
Now it was my turn to say something.

I felt small and unworthy among these mature people,
experts at their work, educated people who had travelled a
long, hard road.

I extricated myself by asking a question, which seemed to
me both mature, and valid.

'What is missing in this tent? We are gathered here as a
community of faith. We have prayed together. As though we
were early Christians, we have received one of our number
into the Church, who from now on will walk in faith, trying
to live in imitation of Jesus, our Lord and Teacher.

'But what is missing in this tent? Tell me!'

A voice, Francesco's, broke the silence: 'The Eucharist.
The presence of Jesus under the sign he left us at the Last
Supper.'

I said nothing.

Never had I felt as at that moment the historical absurdity
of a community of Christians deprived of the Eucharist for
the sole reason that no priest was present.

But the priest was far away. It had been many months
since these prospectors had received Communion, for lack of
priests. All were militant Christians, conscientious about their
faith, and it was only because their work and their duties had
taken them so far away that they were forced to live without
the Eucharist for months on end.

In that tent, and seeing that community gathered there, hundreds of kilometres from the nearest mission – I realized that the situation was really unjustifiable.

Why? Why did communities in Zaire or Equatorial Guinea, made up of excellent Christians instructed by their African catechists, have to go without the Eucharist simply because they had no priest?

Why did they have no priest? Because those people were all married, and the Church only ordained celibates.

Could it really be that celibacy should constitute the absolute *sine qua non*?

Could it really be that merely being married debarred one from consecrating the Body of the Lord in the assembly of the faithful?

Was this what Jesus commanded?

Was being married so great a defect, as to rule out the possibility of becoming a priest in Christ's Church?

No, no, there was something wrong here! Something amiss in the Church's attitude today.

Clearly, it was the weight of a past already over and done, and would have to be faced up to. It was obedience to an out-moded historical situation, which continued to operate by exploiting either the indolence of the faithful, which is great, or the mysterious power that taboos have in age-old traditions and myth-based cultures.

What had Jesus' will been in instituting the Eucharist?

Had he commanded celibacy, or had he commanded, 'Do this in memory of me'?

Had not the will to celibacy, driven to the most improbable extremes in recent centuries, especially by religious, ended by distorting the very will of Christ?

Between an obligatory celibacy reducing the number of priests, and the need not to have the community without the Eucharist, which is the right choice to make?

Hasn't the community a right to the Eucharist?

Why deny it to them merely because they have no celibate willing to be a priest?

I once saw a letter, written by an African, an exemplary

Christian and father, to his bishop, which read more or less as follows:

Father Bishop:

I should like to ask you a favour. Our village is entirely Christian, but it is very, very small. And it will never be able to have a permanent priest to celebrate daily Mass, as we should like. Sometimes we have to wait for months before having the joy of Mass.

Father Bishop, we have our catechist among us. He is married, he is good, he is rich in faith and charity. Why not ask the Pope to give you the power to ordain him a priest?

This way we shall always have the Eucharist.

What answer can be given to this poor Christian?

What logical reasons are there for refusing his request?

Is it enough, everlastingly to repeat that the priesthood can be conferred only on celibates?

Why not on married people as well?

Is there any prohibition in Scripture?

What was done in the primitive Church?

How were things managed in the early centuries?

Or perhaps haven't we, whether by historical necessity or because of our celibate tastes, changed the order of things? I think so.

I speak as a celibate, from a celibacy given me by God himself as an irreversible charism.

I discern in myself no other alternative in life and have such joy in my body by reason of this gift entrusted to me by the Lord, that I venture to say, with Paul, 'Brothers and sisters, I wish you were all like me.'

But with just as much force and awareness, I tell you that I could wish to have received the Eucharist from my father, who was well worthy of being a priest even though he was married.

With just as much hope, I assure you that we are on the eve of a time when the Church will stop making the customary speeches about the shortage of priests today, because these speeches are not true. There is no shortage of priests today.

We have all we need, and more than we need – as always, thanks to God's generous provision for us.

But they are to be found among married people, and that is where the Church should look for them.

What a change it will be to stop feeling worried about the shortage of priests in the Church!

What a joy it will be when the Church at large realizes that things have changed, and that the closing of the seminaries for celibates only, which God himself has emptied, has been a grace, one of the greatest graces of post-Conciliar times.

If I may be allowed to say so!

9 A Taboo to Be Rid Of

Years have passed, and I still think about that baptism, conferred in remotest Africa, so rich in terms of human faith and maturity, and yet so poor because of the irrational eucharistic fast.

But more frequently, and certainly more emphatically, I keep asking myself: Why?

Even today, when we have a pope like John Paul, with his talent for inspiring married couples when he speaks of conjugal love as itself being an experience of God's love, we still see the Church, God's Church, stuck in a past infinitely remote from the universal, radical and explosive reality of today.

I wonder whether Pope John Paul would be nervous about ordaining his trade unionist friend Lech Walesa a priest so that he could celebrate Mass among his workmates?

Well, I know the answer. In Poland there are all those celibate priests, there is no need to ordain married men.

Yes, this is true, but can the same be said for Brazil or for African countries?

I have known communities wait for months to have the Eucharist.

Is this just?

But now we're back in our minor key, sounding the note so offensive to a whole category of people.

To be nervous about ordaining a married man to the priesthood means basically having no confidence in the married state. It means – and this is God's own truth – by implication that the celibate state is the true, the only, state of perfection in the Church.

And this is false.
This is a taboo.

I know I have touched on a delicate point.

I know that some people will be scandalized.

I am sorry about that, but I cannot keep silent.

And besides, I do speak as a celibate. So I have my own papers in order, and I can say this.

I told you, and I repeat that the Lord asked me to accept the charism of virginity, and that when I thank him for the gift he has given me, I weep for joy.

I am happy in the solitude of my cell. He himself is my pillow, my intimacy, my fullness, my spouse.

But I cannot bear it when the Church hints that my state is 'special' – a special kind of perfection.

No, perfection is in charity, not in celibacy.

I have met many, many married people who are richer in love, in self-giving, in prayer, in union with God, than I am.

It is an ugly taboo from the past to judge people by their civil status and not look at what really matters: faith, hope and charity.

And in this, celibacy is not what counts, any more than it is marriage that misses the mark.

We have come to a pretty pass when we say, 'There are no priestly vocations', when world and Church are full of priestly vocations.

To be sure, you will no longer find vocations in 'yesterday's seminaries'. But you can find all you want in 'today's seminaries' – movements, like the Neo-Catechumenal Way communities, Catholic Action, the Focolare, the Comunione e liberazione groups, the Cursillo movement – in other words, all those communities within the Church that are in earnest about their journey in faith, that do not discriminate between people on the grounds of anything as intimate as celibacy, which modesty and discretion should forbid us to whisper or talk about.

Instead of reopening the minor seminaries – which were a real educational disgrace and a desperate effort to influence the young in conditions far removed from that freedom of charisms which God alone bestows – the Church should let the young get their training in the normal interchange of parish life, and above all in the communities of faith and prayer.

In this environment, which is 'in the world', but does not 'belong to the world' (cf. John 17:11, 16), young people can find their own way in life, can become aware of their individual charism, take the road in faith and love with their contemporaries, serve the community by their commitment – and either get married or not, depending on their calling.

And when the need arises for a priest in a community, let the bishop select one from a much broader spectrum than that of the usual celibates.

Is there anything in the gospel contrary to this way of going about things?

Is there anything so very strange in the notion that your own father could give you the Eucharist?

There are some difficulties here, raised by those who are bound to the past, and I should like to say something about those.

The first is the concept of the priest as a 'one-man act'.

The first objection runs as follows: If the bishop ordained a married man, how could the latter devote himself to the common good as unreservedly as a celibate can? Busy with his own professional and family duties, how could he attend to catechism classes, church services, and that whole hurly-burly of parish life?

True. If the community is a community of corpses, of people who expect the priest to do everything, who put all the burden on his shoulders, then it is no use even thinking about a change like this. Indeed it would be harmful.

But if the community is a living community, where catechism is dealt with by mothers and fathers, and where everyone takes on apostolic responsibility, what is left for the priest to do?

Precisely what the primitive Church said he would do after the institution of the diaconate: This will allow us to 'devote ourselves to prayer and to the service of the word' (Acts 6:4)!

But the big difficulty is a different one, and is perhaps the real reason why the Church has been so fanatically attached to the transmission of authority to celibates: the parish benefice.

Yes, the priest's benefice.

It may seem strange, a trifle materialistic, but . . .

I have heard it said: It is hard to support a priest as it is. What would it be like if we had to support priests' families too – including their grandchildren (for which the old Latin word is *nepotes*)?

This argument takes the bull by the horns and the very mention of nepotism, which prevailed in the Middle Ages at all levels, particularly the highest ones, disarms the innovators forthwith.

No, let's stick with the lesser evil. Let's be content with our celibates, even if they are scarce . . . and distorted.

The problem has shifted now. The real problem is not about vocation but about the community. If you have a community of do-nothing Christians, who expect the priest to do everything, inevitably you will have to pay him, and probably stay in the category of dead churches, or those only alive on Sundays for a little worship, to maintain the illusion that by so doing you won't end up in hell.

But if you have a living community, in which each and every baptized person learns to be involved as though he were a priest, then you could do without a priestly benefice. Or better, the benefice would be for the poor, not for the priest.

The priest should live by his work, like everyone else.

If I were a bishop I would only ordain men who were economically self-supporting.

The step to be taken is truly a giant one, for once the priest starts asking the community only to give of themselves, as Paul did, the climate will totally change, and the gospel will be proclaimed not on the basis of stipends or envelopes, but under the impulse of the Spirit.

After all, do Catholic Action militants, the Focolare, the Neo-Catechumenal Way communities, the leaders of Comunione e liberazione, the tireless missionaries of Renewal, the

members of the Voluntariato – do these ask you for a stipend
when they work, when they run meetings, when they spend
all night over the duplicating machine?

If simple lay people give this example of Christians capable
of earning their own living and still having time left over for
the parish, why shouldn't the same example be set by the
parish priests?

And let us keep well in mind: If someone has too much to
do and hasn't got time to earn his living, the real reason
nearly always is that he is overdoing things or, worse, trying
to do everything himself.

Accredited Bible scholars, theologians, bishops, missionaries at home and abroad, are a case apart. But such cases
are not to be multiplied, and the community should be
conscious of its duty to support them.

Like Paul, that extreme protagonist of service to the
Church, each of us should be able to boast of not being a
burden on the churches, as Paul boasted and worked to set
an example.

And when there was a collection to be taken up, or
discussed, to help certain churches that had been impoverished by famine, he was certainly prepared to do it now and
then, for particular cases. But not for clerical endowments.

Yes, make no bones about it. The real danger for the
churches is wealth and property, real insults to the poverty
of Christ and real snares for Christians.

Endowments give rise to jealousy. They alienate from the
primitive enthusiasm of the gospel. And worst of all, they
have to be defended by worldly means: compromise, capita-
lism, usury and even worse.

When I saw the seminaries and novitiates emptying after the
pontificate of Pius xii, I was literally terrified. Then, as Jesus
invites us to do in such cases, I prayed.

And that was when I seemed to understand, confusedly at
first, but then more and more clearly, that with a phenomenon
so vast we ought to look more closely, and see whether, down
deep, there isn't something that God is trying to tell his
Church.

It was not a question of this or that seminary, of this or that region, but of all the seminaries. The whole Church was afflicted with the same problem.

When I think how my Cardinal spent ten years of work – and what work! – bleeding the diocese to build a seminary which looked like a tourist village, and then found it empty almost as soon as it was finished, I said to myself, in my incurable simplicity: 'Either God is playing a joke on us, or he means to teach us a lesson we won't forget!'

And when I saw new, empty seminaries in Rovigo, Bologna, Santo Lussurgiu, Assisi, Fermo, Brescia, Turin, Verona, Vicenza, and so on . . .!

I do not believe the Lord would wish to play jokes on his Church. No, he must have wished to say, in a somewhat blunt way, that it ought to change vocation strategy.

For it is unthinkable that God would want to leave his Church without priests.

It would be a serious lack of faith to think that.

Let us not forget: the priest is bound to the eucharistic mystery, and I cannot do without the Eucharist.

Well, then?

Well, then I became convinced that the simultaneous closing of all the seminaries was only an 'organizational problem', due to the unforeseeable strategy of the Spirit.

God had new seminaries already in mind: today's.

And which ones are they?

I know something about them, having lived in them, having constantly seen them being born, and seen fortune smile on their development. But I never had imagined they would be so important.

Now I do think so! The seminaries of today are the movements springing up in the Church.

As Francis founded the Franciscans, so Chiara Lubich founds the Focolare. As Dominic founded the Dominicans, so Chico Arguello founds the Neo-Catechumenal Way communities. As Ignatius . . . so Giussani founds Comunione e liberazione.

Try it and see. Go to a Mariapolis, or to a Voluntariato meeting. Take part in a few Catholic Action meetings. Enter into the secrets of Opus Dei, or pass a few hours in prayer with Spiritual Renewal groups.

Ask a question.

Try asking: which of you would be willing to be a priest, to work in the community as a priest, to accept the burdens and toil of being a priest?

A forest of hands will go up.

Doctors, teachers, office workers, labourers, engineers, artists . . . many, many hearts in the Church today have developed the charism of priest, of servant and pastor.

And to none of those who raise their hand will it have occurred to respond in the hopes of making a career of it, of getting a benefice, of being served by others.

This is a fact.

I can tell you this because I have tried it. I have asked, I have spoken, I have heard. There is no shortage of priests in the Church today. Do not tell the big fib: 'There is a shortage of priests.' It is not true.

There is a shortage of celibates, not a shortage of priests!

Is it a sin not to be celibate?

Is it a defect in human nature?

The priesthood is a service, and a service can be rendered either by a celibate or by a married man.

The choice belongs to the bishop, and wouldn't it be better if he could choose from a larger number of candidates?

Wouldn't this be an advantage?

The important thing is not to choose from those looking for a benefice, but from those volunteering to serve the community, those who know how to give, not from those who have nothing else to do or who do not know what to do with themselves.

And if these huge seminaries you have built prey on your mind as they become empty, I have a suggestion as to what you might do with them. First, do not sell them. They are still usable. Only – well, they will be used in a different way.

When I got the idea of writing this book, as always, I looked for a peaceful place where I could pray and work in silence. I found an old Dominican house at Taggia on the Ligurian Sea, a wonderful, enormous house, built for hundreds of religious who are no longer there. The ones who remain, a lively, intelligent group, have very rightly not got rid of it but have given it new life. The whole coast profits from it. There is a never-ending succession of prayer courses, encounters and retreats. Particularly, it has become the centre for Cursillos de Cristianidad. Yes, this enchanting place has become a centre for encounter and prayer. A marvellous thing!

Once there were fifty Dominicans in this house. Today there are hundreds of other 'Dominicans' in lay clothes, but living the same mystery of Christ in their homes, and thus expanding and diversifying the effectiveness of the old house, now fresh, young and alive again as it was in days gone by.

One last thing and perhaps the most serious, or anyhow what inspired me to write about this problem. I don't want to upset anyone, still less do I want to talk to a blank wall.

The *problem* of celibacy.

This worries me. Not a day passes when my monastic cell does not hear the anguish of priests, who come to complain about the problems of a celibacy poorly understood, poorly borne and poorly lived.

The virginal, mystical priesthood is not something very widespread among the majority of priests today. Caught up in the whirl of parish activity, in constant, casual contact with women, virtually without private prayer, often wealthy and comfortable, they cannot cope with a 'ministerial' celibacy.

As diocesan priests for the most part live today, I would say that true, mystical, joyous, uplifting, creative celibacy has become something exceptional.

But how is it that the Church does not see these things?

How do the bishops put up with such double standards and, not least, with such wrecks of men, crushed by the weight of a merely juridical celibacy?

And on and on it goes.

The talk is ever of vocational recruiting, covering the same old ground as has yielded such bitter experiences in the past. The dioceses – particularly the ones that built these colossal seminaries – instead of wondering why, after such exhaustive efforts and such expenditure, the Lord should have rewarded their pains in so niggardly a manner by burdening them with the worry of all these huge, empty buildings, with these gaunt groups of candidates inside – instead of changing course, have begun discussing whether or not to reopen the minor seminaries!

Isn't there un-wisdom in all this? Or does prophecy no longer reside in our dioceses?

And what can we say about people who concentrate all their energies on how young people seem to have nothing to do nowadays, or how difficult it is for them to get into the mainstream of life – and who gather little groups of insecure young men, and boys who do not know what to do with themselves and who enter the seminary mainly to solve their scholastic difficulties or often because they have nothing to eat?

'Something will come out of it, even if not much', these people think; without realizing that they are exploiting poverty, when seeking by every means to cobble up something or other and prove that the seminary still has life in it, rather than admit that that system is done for.

For my part, when I wanted to sort out my own thoughts on the subject, I went to stay for a while with future candidates for the priesthood, those spare little groups of students in fourth- and fifth-year theology, on whom all hopes are pinned for solving the problem of vocations . . .

Well, it was right there, with them, that I decided to write what I'm writing.

It was these few who convinced me what a mistake it was to adopt this approach.

For these few themselves are going through a crisis. They themselves admit to the 'trouble they have in deciding'.

And their uneasiness is not about accepting ordination. It is about accepting celibacy.

There is sadness here. And sometimes dishonesty!

No, when you see the way Christianity is organized today, the way prayer is lived in religious houses, the comfort of Christians' lives you realise that mystical celibacy is only a theory, rarely verified in practice, and certainly not often enough to meet the Church's need for an enormous number of priests.

Yes, I am convinced: God has personally emptied the seminaries because he wants something else. And we must look for this something else in simplicity of heart and freedom of spirit.

Above all, I think God no longer wants obligatory celibacy.

I believe in celibacy too much to see it reduced to such a sorry state.

And there is only one way to save it: leave it to free choice, humbly begging it as a gift from above, as a charism that only the God of the impossible can give.

The day the choice is free, and the priesthood is possible in either state, the number of celibates will increase, since the Church will have proved that it does not place its trust in itself and attribute to itself, as heretofore, the power to create celibates, but looks for them to God alone.

And if grace so abounds as to produce in the Church the miracle of enough celibates to assure the priestly ministry, we shall certainly sing the Magnificat. But we shall never return – and this is basic to the spirituality of marriage – we shall never return to the notion that when one gets married one becomes a mediocre Christian.

Just a few more words to conclude this chapter, which may have alarmed some people by its directness.

I am under no illusions.

I have known the Church since I was a lad. Since the day God's goodness called me to follow Christ, I have had no other dream than to serve the Body of Christ, which is the Church. Without boasting, I can say that few missionaries have travelled more kilometres than I. I have travelled road after road, to reach even the smallest villages and parishes lost in the mountains.

I have worked in international movements. I have seen all the continents.

I have gone into monasteries and seminaries, to gather whatever I could there.

And I have not travelled the world as a sightseer, but only for the joy of praying in liturgical assemblies and sharing in whatever was stirring the Church.

I repeat, I am under no illusions and understand the scope of the proposal that I as a member of the Church have just made bold to make.

I know too that the majority of parishes are still bound to the past, hence to the same sort of worship, clericalism and priests that we have seen, century after century.

If changes occurred in these places it would be a disaster.

My own mother, or my sisters, whose faith, zeal and loyalty to the Church I can warrant, would be scandalized to see the village doctor, a married man with four children, appear in the sanctuary to preside at the Eucharist.

We must take account of taboos and the enormous influence of tradition on the masses.

Changes cannot be made suddenly, especially in matters already inflamed by controversy, such as celibacy and the exclusion of married men from the government of the Church.

This will need time and, more particularly, changes in the concept of the Church as the people of God, and of the parish as the community and not as the private property of a man known as the parish priest.

But we might make a start by thinking and praying about it. We might make a start by calmly examining the situation and not being scandalized if a woman reads part of the liturgy at Mass, or if, among the acolytes round the priest, we begin to see, with the boys we are used to, a few grave little girls as well.

The real revolution will be carried out at grassroots level, by communities of faith, who are accustomed to reading the Word – by communities who are making a journey of faith, and who themselves with their increasingly mature and balanced view will get into the habit of indicating to the bishop the future candidates for the ministry of the liturgy.

This is bound to happen. But it should be given mature consideration by pastors of the Church as they become more and more accustomed to living with prayer communities, far away from cathedrals, among the workers and peasants.

The process of transformation will actually begin in the countries of Africa, Asia and Latin America, where for a long time already the Christian congregations have been held together by the faith of lay people, not of priests. The latter become accustomed to turning up at the last minute, to say Mass, and not to evangelize since they have no time for this, consumed as they are by their haste to . . . say Mass.

And if you want a piece of advice, especially today, now that people have become so very sensitive about witness, about truth, about free service . . . see to it that money ceases altogether to have any connection with holy things.

This will be the only way, and it will be a radical one, for Christians no longer need to found banks or to submit, albeit unwillingly, to the mighty.

And in case anyone who recalls God's word only when convenient maintains that even the apostle Paul defended the right to 'live by the altar', do not be afraid to reply that 2000 years have passed since then, and that the modern world, with its technology and maturity, knows perfectly well how to obtain what the community needs, without inflicting the humiliation on it of seeing a priest getting paid for a Mass or any other liturgical rite.

At least you should strike a blow for decency!

Surely you are aware of the incongruity, and often venal nastiness, of the sacristy, or of the irrational way in which the regular administration of a Christian community is conducted, shrouded in mystery?

Don't these things strike you as leftovers from the past?

10 We Are All Priests, Men and Women Alike

In studying the truly exceptional life of St Francis of Assisi, I linger with particular interest over his personal motives for not wishing to be ordained a priest.

It is funny how all the painters show him so insistently in priestly vestments. Actually, though, the most classic pictures of him that have come down to us show a Francis at prayer, with arms uplifted, as if seeking to offer to the Almighty, his Good Lord, the creatures of the whole visible and invisible universe, feeling himself to be their offerer, their voice, their song.

Now, why did Francis not wish to be a priest?

Out of humility, is the answer most people give me.

How strange! Then Pope John, who did want to be a priest – was he not humble enough? The Curé d'Ars, so little, so small, was he lacking in humility, in wanting to become a priest at any price?

No, I find this humility business unconvincing. Humility is truth, the highest truth, and those who feel deep down inside that they want to serve their fellow-man as priests are not, I think, lacking in humility. Quite the reverse!

Then, why?

I have found an answer which has been very helpful to me, and I thank the great Umbrian for it.

Francis did not want to be a priest because he had the particular charism of developing in the Church one of the greatest mystical ideals of all times – an ideal which, being too beautiful, invariably risks being shoved out of sight and even out of mind: this ideal of the priesthood of all the baptized, known in theological parlance as the 'priesthood of the faithful'.

For that matter, even as inspirer and founder of religious orders, he was always preoccupied with this same central ideal which had inspired him. He did not assemble a community of priests, though some priests did follow him. He did not found an order in which the clergy had the preponderance and determined the tone.

No, absolutely not.

The greater number of his followers were called 'brothers'. They were simple laymen, thirsting for a consecrated life, and they continued being what they had always been: farmers, craftsmen, clerks, labourers.

After all, in the tradition of Western monasticism, deriving its inspiration from Benedict, this same path had been trodden for centuries. In a Benedictine monastery, the majority of the monks were not priests. The liturgical ministry was the responsibility of the abbot and his associates: the great mass of religious were never ordained priests. Their charism was working in the fields, making bread, weaving wool, building walls, reclaiming marshes, discharging the common tasks of the monastery.

The characteristic mark set by Francis on Western monasticism was that of a more drastic and socially evident poverty, but he did not alter the structure of the religious life of his times which was quite distinct from that of the clergy and their pastoral functions at diocesan and parochial level.

It was only later, and not without resistance, that monks, and even the *Poverelli* themselves, became more or less completely clericalized.

The parishes gained here, for now they began to have religious as their pastors. But the religious charism was very much the loser, losing its primitive force.

Anyhow, be the historical side of the matter as it may, this helped me to think of Francis as a saint who said to me: I am not a priest, but when I offer myself and the creatures around me to my Most High Lord I profoundly feel myself to be someone who offers sacrifice.

Go and do likewise. And explain this to those with their

feet in the mud of the ricefields, to those who toil at the drudgery of desk work, and to those with a house full of children and worries.

Let us never forget: in baptism we all become priests, and from these priests, these true priests, anyone ordained by the bishop, in Christ's name, to serve the Church, is chosen.

How easy it would be to explain all this if we used terms properly. We do not use them properly, and this has never ceased to amaze me.

All we should have to do would be to say:

1   The whole people of God is a priestly people;
2   Every baptized person is a priest;
3   The community has need of leaders, shepherds, heads, celebrants, and these we call the presbyters. They are selected and ordained by the bishop to serve the entire priestly people.

How I should love to see this form 'priest', which says so little, fall gradually into disuse and be replaced by the truer, more mature term, 'presbyter'.

But . . .

Let me explain more clearly what I mean.

I became an active member of the Church as a boy, and while, owing to my nature, I was not always a good Christian, I always attended to what was being said and thought in the Church.

I have always found it easy to absorb the culture circulating in our churches: the thought patterns, the more evident traditions, the more influential emphases. But I must admit, I have never heard an accurate presentation of the theory of the priesthood. To me as a boy, as a lad and then as a militant Christian, the concept of priesthood was only ever explained to me in relationship to the ministerial priesthood.

I was long convinced that the only priesthood was the clerical one, and that the priestly task had been assigned, as in antiquity, to the 'tribe of Levi'.

That is, just as in the Old Testament the twelve tribes of Israel selected one particular tribe to lead its worship, so in the New Testament . . . and so on.

This concept was so deeply rooted in me that I had

difficulty in understanding what Rosmini meant in his book *The Five Wounds of the Church*.

Once I did understand, I felt very, very upset.

How could there be this silence about the priestly nature of the whole people of God? What danger would the Church of Jesus run by forcefully affirming that all the baptized – men and women, great and small, wise or ignorant – are full-fledged priests?

Absolutely each and every one!

Sinners too!

And this not by merit of theirs, but because they are grafted on to Christ by baptism, so that in him, they become saints, prophets and priests.

As it is written: You are a people of saints, you are a people of prophets, you are a people of priests (cf. 1 Peter 2:9).

Is this true or not?

Is this a piece of pious and devout sentimentality, or is it a theological truth?

Why, then, preach so insistently on the unique greatness of those to be ordained priests by the bishop?

Thereby giving the impression – and not just the impression, either – that the laity are the pariahs of the Church and count for nothing?

Rosmini wrote that one of the 'wounds of the Church' was that of having partitioned the priestly people, composed of all the baptized, thus dividing them into two churches: dividing the ministerial priests from the rest of the laity and so constructing a church with a Church.

And the result?

No longer accorded the dignity due to them and inadequately nourished on the word of God summoning them to holiness and prophecy, the laity gradually became a dead weight, an anonymous crowd, incapable of assuming any real responsibility in the Church.

Go to a meeting on vocations and you will immediately see where the real emphasis lies.

Incredibly, you will hear that what counts for the Church is the ministerial priesthood; and all energy and aspiration will be concentrated on that.

And everything else?

Everything else is a filler, an anonymous herd.

Milch-cows for when money is wanted.

A panorama of heads to which reproofs and sage advice are addressed.

Thank you, Francis, who by not being a ministerial priest yourself, helped me to understand that I too could be a priest in a genuine, theological sense, without being one in the ministerial sense.

Because I too went through this crisis, and did not want to be ordained a priest.

For different reasons, I admit. Reasons that were authentic signs of my own times.

Not, certainly, out of humility. I did not want to be a priest, for reasons to do with the apostolate. I got my training during the pontificate of Pius XII, when, under the impulse of Catholic Action, the laity began to be aware of their dignity in the service of the Church.

This was the great inspiration of Pope Pacelli, a pope particularly sensitive to the dignity of the laity and to their involvement in the field of the apostolate.

It was an epic breakthrough for us, and each of us felt understood and helped.

It was then, right then, during my time in Catholic Action, that I decided not to be ordained a priest, thus leaving me free to proclaim, in lay clothes, to the laity as yet ignorant and unaware, that the Church was the Church of all, and not only of the priests – as the parishes of that time largely gave the impression.

We were all part of the Church, and all had to feel that the Church belonged to us, and work at spreading the Kingdom by our own activity, which was beginning to take on the face of an authentic personal vocation.

These were marvellous times, and I thank God for letting me live in them.

I must, however, say that we had not yet fulfilled our aim. We were still on the way.

Fulfilment was to come with the Council.

What an illumination for all of us it was, when the Council stood the theology of the Church on its head in its efforts to 'rethink itself as Church', as Pope John liked to put it, and later defined itself so clearly with Pope Paul.

The Church was a clerical pyramid no more. It was the people of God, marching through the desert; a society of faith and prayer, in which each one had his place; the mystery of Christ alive in history, the people whom Christ had won by his blood and to whom he had transmitted, by his Spirit on Calvary, holiness, prophecy and priesthood.

It was the Church of the new age.

The new age has arrived, and it is ours.

Perhaps it is the beginning of the end-time, announced by the prophet Joel:

> . . . I will pour out my spirit on all mankind.
> Your sons and daughters will prophesy,
>   your old men will dream dreams,
>   and your young men see visions.
> Even on the slaves, men and women,
>   will I pour out my spirit in those days (Joel 3:1–2).

And Jeremiah says the same in broader terms:

> See, the days are coming – it is Yahweh who speaks – when I will make a new covenant with the house of Israel (and the house of Judah), but not a covenant like the one I made with their ancestors on the day I took them by the hand to bring them out of the land of Egypt. They broke that covenant of mine, so I had to show them who was master. It is Yahweh who speaks. No, this is the covenant I will make with the House of Israel when those days arrive – it is Yahweh who speaks. Deep within them I will plant my Law, writing it on their hearts. Then I will be their God and they shall be my people. There will be no further need for neighbour to try to teach neighbour, or brother to say to brother, 'Learn to know Yahweh!' No, they will all know me, the least no less than the greatest . . . (Jeremiah 31:31–4).

These new times are Christ's times.

He is the one, eternal Priest.

The ancient priesthood has been abolished; under the New Covenant he is the one, eternal Priest.

But in his mercy, he has willed to associate his people with him, a people he has won, the Church.

And the Church is no other than the Body of the Lord.

And every part of it shares in his life, without distinction.

Is he holy? Then we are holy.

Is he a prophet? Then we are prophets.

Is he a priest? Then we are priests.

We are his people, a people of saints, prophets and priests.

The great sacrament is baptism, and in baptism we are grafted on to Christ for ever.

In him we die, in him we rise.

Henceforth our greatness is the sap that flows into us from his living trunk.

We cannot be detached from him any more. Doesn't the apostle say:

Nothing therefore can come between us and the love of Christ, even if we are troubled or worried, or being persecuted, or lacking food or clothes, or being threatened or even attacked . . . nothing can ever come between us and the love of God made visible in Christ Jesus, our Lord (cf. Romans 8:35, 39).

All else flows from this extraordinary fact.

Christ is my soul.

Christ is my strength.

Christ is my holiness.

Christ is my prophecy.

Christ is my priesthood.

In him we are enabled to do something impossible for human beings: to offer ourselves to the Father in holy oblation.

This is the sum and synthesis of all: the ability to offer oneself to the Father. This is the very soul of priesthood.

Being able to offer oneself to God as an act of love.

And each of us is a priest, in proportion to this ability, which only the Holy Spirit can confer.

Then the rest will follow: public worship will follow, the ministerial priesthood will follow, ordination for the service of the community will follow and so forth.

But the sum of all, the unifying force of all, lies in the ability conferred by the Holy Spirit on the baptized, in Jesus' death, to become like Jesus: an offering of oneself to the Father.

If only my mother had known that, how happy she would have been!

But she did not, since the catechism of her day had not told her.

And so, at home, she would go on saying: How happy I should be if a son of mine were a priest!

She did not know that what really counted was for herself and her children to be priests in Christ.

And you *were* one, dear Mother!

Forgive me, friends, for giving way to emotion.

What I should be saying is that this discovery had a great influence on me as a member of the Church, and not a few hard words have escaped my lips against the ill-made, incomplete catechisms of my time.

Now I feel at peace, and the Council, with its definition of the Church as the people of God, has been of real help to me.

And I feel at peace with the latest adult catechism put out by the Italian Bishops' Conference.

How mature it is!

What a joy to read!

11 We Like to Count Ourselves

When I was young, and things were going badly, I used to hear the parishioners say: 'Let's have a nice procession'.

When I grew up, and things were going worse, there was always someone in the diocese to suggest enthusiastically: 'We ought to have a big rally.'

Now I am old, and things go worse than ever, the solution seems to be: big meetings.

And there we are, always back at square one.

Strange, the need we feel to count ourselves.

It is as though, weakened by our deficiencies, we seek a cure-all in singing hymns as loud as we can in the public square.

It is as though, worried by our spiritual emptiness, we seek security in strength of numbers, like a little tonic to buck you up when you feel frail.

It would seem however, that things are no different to the past, and that on this topic too we can say with the ancients: There is nothing new under the sun.

Whether it is Constantine, or Charlemagne, or Heraclius impassioned for his crusades, it is the same thing all over again. Alarmed at the harshness of the faith and the cross, we look for help in a political project.

Unable to believe in what the Word says: 'our help is in the name of Yahweh, who made heaven and earth' (Psalm 124:8), we settle for affirming: 'My help is in the name of ———————— [enter name of country, legislator, influential member of business community or crook], who will certainly give me a helping hand.'

One would have thought the people of God in ancient times

had already been taught a clear lesson, couched in searing terms, but . . . it is so easy to forget.

The Bible relates how David, towards the end of his reign, took it into his head to count his people's military resources, and gave orders to have a census taken. Naturally, Joab's warning was not enough to stop him. Joab had warned him that Yahweh alone 'kept the records', that is, the true ones, but David decided to carry out his arrogant project anyway.

When the census was over, poor David, having disobeyed God, who had not wanted the count to be taken, heard these words from Gad, speaking in Yahweh's name: I offer you three things; . . . three years of famine to come on your country . . . or will you flee for three months before your pursuing enemy, or would you rather have three days' pestilence in your country? (2 Samuel 24:12–13).

David's choice was not an easy one, and if you want to know how the story ended, you can read it in chapter 24 of the Second Book of Samuel.

The fact is that the disease is within us, and it is not easy to root it out. Not even for popes.

Even the apostles occasionally had the urge to hold a 'meeting' in Jerusalem. But not exactly where Christ wanted it.

The apostles were all out in the streets of the capital – capitals always have the power to attract our attention! – and doubtless a few of them already had their knives under their tunics, as Peter had on that famous dark night in the olive garden, when he drew it and used it to cut off Malchus's ear. (Yes, and if Malchus had kept still, he would have lost something else besides an ear, Peter was so angry.)

Jesus wanted to hold a meeting too, but in somewhat different circumstances from those the Twelve, especially Peter, intended.

Listen to what Jesus says, as Matthew reports it: 'From that time Jesus began to make it clear to his disciples that he was destined to go to Jerusalem and suffer grievously at the hands of the elders and chief priests and scribes, to be put to death . . . (Matthew 16:21).

The gathering proposed by Christ was of a different nature, and the apostolic college had neither the same ideas nor sufficient maturity to understand them.

Besides, who could have come to grips with a total reversal such as Jesus was proposing?

Who could have grasped the project hidden in the ages, and now about to be revealed?

Who could have understood the 'Jesus Project', in which victory is won by losing, in which the believer's strength lies in his weakness (cf. 2 Corinthians 2:9–10), in which happiness resides in poverty and powerlessness, and death is gain (cf. Philippians 1:21)?

I doubt whether even Jesus had any hopes that people who had only recently begun to follow him would be able to grasp the full scope of the mystery contained in his words.

He prepared the ground, when he said: '. . . You cannot bear it now, but when the Spirit of truth comes, he will lead you to the complete truth' (cf. John 16:12–13).

And the Spirit did come, and as if to make himself heard slammed the doors of Jerusalem for good and all. But . . .

Many people are convinced that with the advent of the Church everything now becomes orderly, clear and easy. But that is not the way things are.

Who of us is born into the New Testament?

Who of us has been able to absorb Jesus' thought, especially about the mystery of the cross?

Baptized we may be, but our feet are still firmly anchored in the Old Testament, and we know more about the murmuring in the desert than about the Beatitudes of the New Jerusalem.

It is not easy to accept Jesus in all his breadth and depth. Even the Church finds it a good deal easier to accept the law of the Old Testament than the novelty of the love contained in the New.

At every moment, we are tempted to turn to the security of law. Many things have been quickly grasped right, but not everything.

I am sure that, on this earth, we shall never be able to get to the very bottom of Jesus' thinking!

We try . . .

Some things we understand, some things we do not understand . . .

Some things we understand at the beginning of life, some things at the end.

Some things we understand in the third century of the Church, and some things we start understanding in the twentieth century.

It is a journey. It is the journey of the people of God, but still a journey.

And if you are not convinced, read the history of the Church. You will see that Ayatollah Khomeini is not the only person to have been capable of slaughtering anyone who did not think as officialdom thought.

But I no longer get so furious. The Spirit has given me the grace of seeing my own sinfulness, which is very, very great, and in doing so has rid me of the wish to look about me and see whether there are any sinners even worse than I.

In all this I have understood one thing: that Christ has saved everyone, and that I would not care for a Church which did not sin, because it would not be mine, it would not resemble me, it would not love me; it would judge me and condemn me. It would be as unpleasant to have around, as all those people who are so wrapped up in themselves and their own virtues that they no longer know how to weep for their sins.

Friends, let us all remember: none of us is born into the New Testament, and even when we are properly baptized, for many a year our feet still have to tramp the land of slavery in Egypt, or the waters of Meribah, or the desert of ordeal.

And worse, and practically for ever, under our skin lurks the desire to *win*, as in that first exodus of the Hebrews.

It is incredible how unable we are to go forward without wanting to knock somebody down, without bulldozing our way through, without regarding someone as . . . our enemy.

This is why we count our own numbers. We want to outnumber the others, we want to get our own way.

We calculate the power of our Church by numbers.

We do not care in the least if, when we block the traffic with a big procession, we make people who do not think as we do, blaspheme because they can't get by . . .

It would not be so bad if our obsession with number, strength and security were honest, true, genuine and dictated by love.

But it isn't.

Deep down, what is at work is pride – a sense of superiority to others, the certitude that we are better, that we have more of the truth.

The first time I joined Muslims in prayer, I heard an old Arab behind me mumble to his neighbour, 'What is this dog of a Christian doing here?' The compliment was meant for me.

Have you ever in your life met anyone, especially someone religious, who would say right out that his Church had not got things straight?

Or a Marxist assert that he had made a mistake?

Or a Catholic say that a Protestant was right?

Or a Jehovah's Witness proclaim in the streets that there might be such a thing as an honest pope?

Or an Englishman admit that a Neapolitan was a better fellow than he was?

Or the *Osservatore Romano* state, even down at the bottom of a page, that a Communist had managed to do something good?

No, you have never encountered any such thing. You have not seen it or read it. Or if perchance you have – everything is possible – you ought to enter it in your notebook as something very rare indeed.

This is why we count ourselves.

We want to be better than the others, we want to have exclusive rights to the truth.

The old ascetical writers, who did not mince words, used to say that the greatest sin was pride. And Dante himself, as the good theologian he tried to be, attired this kind of sin in a lion's skin, since in his day the lion was regarded as invincible for anyone unarmed.

Yes, pride is at work here, and often we fail to detect it, especially if it is of a religious nature.

All we have to do is think of the wars of religion, or the holy wars, examples of which we have seen in our own day in the Middle East.

Thank God, the Council has helped us to mature a little, and not only have we finally come to accept religious freedom, but we have begun to seek honest, sincere dialogue with all.

Once I wrote to Paul VI about a desire of mine: that the Holy See would take steps to found a commission to study relations with the Muslims. He replied: 'Not only with Muslims, but with everyone. We shall hold dialogue even with those who claim to be atheists.'

It is not hard to see why he was a great pope.

But let's get back to meetings, to counting ourselves, to big rallies, to strength.

Don't misunderstand me. I do not intend to point an accusing finger!

I am one of the biggest sinners myself, and I know all about holding rallies on the road to Jerusalem.

No, now that I am old, I feel like laughing, and if you asked me: 'Would you have that rally of the 300,000 Green Berets all over again?' I should say 'Yes.' I would do it again. I couldn't help but do it again.

You have to make mistakes. Let me explain.

When I was working in Catholic Action, I remember, one of our defects – and, not mincing our words, we called it a sin – was 'human respect'.

In plain words, what did that mean?

It meant a very bitter reality for those of us who felt we were on our own, especially in the countryside, and there were plenty of us!

In the schools, we practising Christians were always in the minority. In the factories, we were very rare birds indeed.

For instance, when I was a lad, whether at school or in the district, I always had to fight against the majority.

Public opinion, fashion, the bars, the films, were almost always hostile to Christ and to the Church. Consequently, the association, the group, was a sort of stronghold, a defence, a way of not being swept away in our weakness.

In inveighing against human respect, we were striving to incite our comrades and ourselves to be aware of it, yet not be frightened.

Numbers gave us the impression our convictions had solid backing.

I am not surprised, then, when I hear Comunione e liberazione groups talking, and see how they start their activities in a university or high school.

They are like Peter in the streets of Jerusalem, looking for help, trying not to be afraid.

Everything, or almost everything, in political Christianity, with its offensive and defensive pressures, comes back to this psychological problem.

It is inevitable.

Yet with faith in Christ and joining his following, we ought henceforth to be very clear about one thing, that was revealed by him: in our activities there is something pure, and the danger of something not so pure.

Let me explain.

When we decided to gather in Rome and recite our Creed in St Peter's Square, the thrust was authentic; it was love that directed our thoughts and efforts.

Not even our organization expected that there would be so many of us, and I can say that on that truly holy night, steeped in prayer and faith, the Spirit was present in all his splendour and transparency.

It was not the sin of triumphalism. We did not hold that rally to show we were strong. We were like children, happy there were so many of us, and happy to say 'Thank you' to God.

I can swear it.

So where could evil lurk?

It lurked within us and in anyone else who, seeing how strong we were, forthwith transformed this religious fact into a political project.

If a lovely woman looks at herself in a mirror, this is not

wrong. But if, discovering how beautiful she is, she stays there for hours enjoying the sight, that can be dangerous.

And so it was with us. Seeing our strength, we began to believe in that strength, and this was our weakness and the beginning of our decline.

Friends, life is hard!

The gospel is hard!

Jesus makes terrible demands on us. And not even the Church, the Church itself, the Bride of Christ, is altogether safe from the danger of power, pride, lust and ownership.

Jesus warned us.

So hold your 'meetings'. But always remember that the true 'meeting' is the loneliness of Calvary, and that your real strength will never be in numbers, but in your fidelity to the nakedness of God's word and the cross of Christ.

And while we are on the subject of confessions, I should like to tell you one last thing to end this story.

After the rally, which demonstrated our strength, not a single person warned me of the danger that was infiltrating the organization and threatening to bring with it weakness, self-seeking and calculation.

If I had only met one single person to tell me, in the name of God: 'Watch out, for where you think you're strong, you're weak!'

It was only later, in the desert, that I grasped this, as the word of God gradually showed me the deep significance of Jesus' defeat. 'I . . . make my weaknesses my special boast', Paul told me again and again, 'so that the power of Christ may stay over me . . .' (2 Corinthians 12:9).

Masochism?

Self-martyrdom?

A refusal to stand and fight?

Leaving the way open for Satan to conquer the world so as to be able to say to him, after his sure defeat, 'See, I was right all the time'?

Peace at any price?

Facile compromise?

No, friends, none of the above. But rather, Christ's deepest secret for conquering the world.

Christ does not play with the world's cards, he plays with his own.

And his cards are completely unknown to the Adversary.

'Who could believe what we have heard? . . .' Isaiah asks. '. . . to whom has the arm of Yahweh been revealed?' (Isaiah 53:1).

This is how Jesus wins. Here is his victory rally, his 'meeting':

> Like a sapling he grew up in front of us,
> like a root in arid ground.
> Without beauty, without majesty (we saw him),
> no looks to attract our eyes;
> a thing despised and rejected by men,
> a man of sorrows and familiar with suffering,
> a man to make people screen their faces;
> he was despised and we took no account of him.
>
> And yet ours were the sufferings he bore,
> ours the sorrows he carried.
> But we, we thought of him as someone punished,
> struck by God, and brought low.
> Yet he was pierced through for our faults,
> crushed for our sins.
> On him lies a punishment that brings us peace,
> and through his wounds we are healed . . .
>
> Harshly dealt with, he bore it humbly,
> he never opened his mouth,
> like a lamb that is led to the slaughter-house,
> like a sheep that is dumb before its shearers
> never opening its mouth (Isaiah 53: 2–5, 7).

Here too we could say the same thing to Christ:
　　Masochism?
　　Self-martyrdom?
　　No, friends, no!

Jesus plays his sacrificial card, not to lose the battle, but to win it.

His non-violence is not designed to give the victory to his adversary, Evil, but to confound him utterly, to lay him low with love and convert him completely to the truth.

For, Isaiah concludes the Song of the Servant with this victory:

> If he offers his life in atonement,
> he shall see his heirs . . .
> His soul's anguish over
> he shall see the light and be content.
> By his sufferings shall my servant justify many,
> taking their faults on himself.
>
> Hence I will grant whole hordes for his tribute,
> he shall divide the spoil with the mighty . . . (Isaiah 53:10–12).

Isn't this victory?

Nothing conquers more surely than the cross.

Nothing is mightier than the blood of the innocent.

Jesus has conquered me. I feel that I am his and can never more be anything but his. And I owe this to his strategy of love.

Had he come for me astride a white horse, armed to the teeth, as my childish Old Testament religiosity would have had it, I should have abandoned him.

But when I saw him come to me covered in spittle, bleeding, robed in opprobrium and betrayal, I clasped him to my heart and said to him: I am yours for ever.

Jesus, you have conquered!

No longer do I believe in violence, in force, in power. I believe in the way in which you have loved me and love the world.

Christ, you are truly the Son of God!

You are the Saviour of the world!

You are my All!

12 'Mercy I Desire, Not Sacrifice'

Man's first discovery of God by no means induces the feeling of compassion toward sinners!

On the contrary!

When religions are at the beginning of their history, they are characterized by severity, by harshness – I might indeed say, rage – directed against those who transgress the law, who 'offend God', as they say: not excluding the Jewish religion, the stock from which the Christian religion has sprung as Judaism's flowering and fulfilment.

This is all so evident that it does not require documentation from the texts.

Many people who start reading the Bible without adequate preparation, end by closing the Book in surprise and even fright, at God's apparent harshness where sinners are concerned.

The fact is that the Bible, too, is on a journey, the same journey as the people of God, bearing witness on its way to a progressive discovery of that God who will eventually reveal himself in his fullness and in all his splendour in Christ.

Someone will say, then: 'Let's skip the whole Old Testament and start right away on the New. This way we shan't waste any time.'

But that is not the way things are. You have to accept the route. Truth and love have themselves travelled that road, and you must be patient.

The longer you tarry in the Old Testament, the better you are prepared for the New. The further you travel patiently with Deuteronomy, the better you will understand the gospel. The longer you spend in the desert, the better you will love the Book of Revelation. The more you read of Leviticus, the better you will understand the Letter to the Hebrews. The more attention you pay to Ezekiel, the better you understand the tastes of John. The more of Isaiah you learn by heart, the better you will see the 'photograph' of Jesus in the gospel.

That is the way it is.

And the same obtains as regards God's attitude to sinners.

The more you try to understand the Old Testament's harshness towards transgressors of the law, the better you prepare your heart to accept Jesus' mercy towards sinners.

As a general rule, zeal for the truth and for the things of God, and everything springing from closer contact with him, unleashes in our spirit a desire for the 'exemplary punishment' of transgressors, and what is more, the dream of seeing the impious vanish from the face of the earth.

'God, if only you would kill the wicked! . . .' (Psalm 139:19).

Primitive religions are particularly fierce when it comes to those who stray, and the death penalty affords a quite special pleasure and satisfaction to the pontiffs and defenders of the so-called divine order.

Khomeini is not alone in his fanatical attachment to the law, in sweeping away adulterous women and hauling out a centuries-old rule about stoning them to death, 'as Moses ordered'.

Anyone who becomes religious automatically becomes a supporter of the 'divine' order, and particularly violent against those who disturb it.

Sinners and tax-collectors are much more merciful towards those who sin; not to mention prostitutes, whose tenderness towards those poor beings, alcoholics, and towards human 'trash' in general, is remarkable.

I remember, after I was converted I was a fanatical defender of 'morality', and I would have burned all sinners at the stake, as well as all those who ignored the Sixth Commandment.

It is a very strange thing that, in young and immature Churches, the one sin to be persecuted is the sin against 'morality'.

Next, when Churches start growing up, the violence is unleashed against 'heretics and schismatics'.

Torture and the pyre are used for these, and mercilessness knows no bounds.

If Jews or Christians would humbly and patiently read the history – the true history – of their past, they would be flabbergasted to find themselves the heirs of earlier Jews and Christians who were capable, out of zeal for God, of hacking to pieces, burning and impaling thousands, condemned to death merely for not thinking in every respect as did the officialdom then wielding the power.

In a nutshell: if the Church that Jesus belonged to, the Synagogue of Jerusalem, had no mercy on Jesus himself and served him up to God as a sacrificial dish by crucifying him, this was nothing at all unusual, and many other people were treated in pretty much the same way, doubtless thinking as Jesus himself had said, '. . . the hour is coming when anyone who kills you will think he is doing a holy duty for God' (John 16:2).

A great deal of water will have to flow under the bridge, including the bridges of the Tiber, before the gospel, Jesus' gospel, finally penetrates into the veins of his Church! And many of our guns will backfire, making us turn tail and run.

A bit of terrorism is enough, and you will hear the cry, 'Let's have the death penalty!' A little more shameless immorality, and many people will dream of exemplary sentences and drastic punishments.

There is nothing new . . .

The 'Death to the Sinner' project, and the 'Shoot the Delinquents' project, are inherited from generation to generation and head the list of facile solutions to hard problems.

Indeed, the civil codes of most nations are based on those notions, assuming that this is the way to put things right.

That the innocent will be better protected.

That the family will be safeguarded.

That people will be more moral.

That adultery will be less frequent.

That marriages will be more stable.

The man, Adam, has a head to reason with, a heart to love with, and a will to decide with.

And Adam decides.

But Adam is the man Adam, and acts as Adam.

Adam is not Jesus. Rather, Jesus is the new Adam, who has the guts to say: '. . . it was said: *Eye for eye and tooth for tooth.* But I say this to you . . .' (cf. Matthew 5:21–48).

And he will turn the page.

He, Christ, is the transition from the Old to the New.

He, Christ, is the revelation of a God who had been distorted by our childish fears and our stunted sense of justice and love!

In my spiritual infancy, the sinner enraged me and inspired me with the passion to eliminate, or at least to punish, him. In the maturity of Jesus' revelation, the sinner inspires me with compassion, and calls out to me for mercy.

In point of fact – and why not admit it? – when I was young, I was in favour of the death penalty. Now that I am old I am no longer in favour of it.

But that is not all. When I first became active in the Church and was going through my paces, I did not know the distinction between a defensive war and a holy war. Today, now that I am close to death, I no longer believe in either.

I believe in non-violence.

I believe in the blood of the innocent.

I believe in winning by losing.

I believe in true disarmament.

I believe in the wolf of Gubbio.

I believe in the potential of a people who no longer take up arms even when surrounded by armed peoples.

I believe in prophecy more than in politics.

I believe in Gandhi.

I believe in Martin Luther King.

I believe in Archbishop Romero.

I believe in Pope John Paul, who after two assassination attempts continues to go unarmed among the crowds with his hand raised in greeting.

I believe and hope in the people of Poland, who would

rather go to gaol and go on protesting and losing their jobs, than make bombs and hunt down their oppressors.

What an example it would be, if a people were to succeed in conquering by force of non-violence alone, without shedding their enemy's blood!

And how I pray this may happen, to redeem Catholics from their past violence – a little.

On a religious level, which is the true, more mature level, the important thing for me is what Jesus said; and I do, or at least I try to do, what Jesus did.

The man Adam can teach me how a car is built, how surgery is performed and how to steer a spaceship.

Jesus teaches me how to enter the kingdom that is his kingdom.

When the choice lies between a civil law prescribing the death penalty for someone who strikes me, and Jesus who tells me to turn the other cheek, I know which to conform to in my heart.

Between a civil law that gaols an adulteress, and Jesus' manner of treating the adulterous woman in the gospel, I know how to choose, even though it may scandalize a few of the devout.

I don't cheat at cards, and I know how to behave.

And if I happen to be living in a country where adulterous women are gaoled, I visit the adulterous women in gaol and take them some fruit. But if I live in a free country, where I can express my opinion at the ballot box, I let the adulterous women out of gaol, with their freedom to sin . . . even though their sinning may upset me very, very much.

What I have tried to do in this book is sum up, for my friends, and for those who want to seek God, the route that I have travelled.

I originally intended to call my book 'Experience of God, Experience of the Church' but this was replaced by the idea given me by Augusto Guerriero, which is clearer; hence the present title: *I Sought and I Found*.

Well, indeed, what have I found?

I shall tell you very briefly.

In the vertical of God's Absolute, in contemplation I have found God.

Yes, contemplation gave me not only the experimental certitude of his existence, but the warmth of his presence, and the marvel of his deeds in the history of mankind and the inexhaustible dynamics of evolution.

And on the horizontal of the human? On the crossbar that stands for relationships with man, with the human family, with my brothers and sisters and everyone, I have found mercy!

What convinced me of the existence of God was contemplation.

What convinced me of his life and his heart was mercy.

I turned completely to God in prayer, and I discovered his inmost essence in his capacity to forgive.

The grandest thing I can say about God is that he is merciful, and I believe in universal salvation.

God's capacity for love, his thirst for justice, his battle against evil, his desire to embrace mankind like a prodigal son – joined to the power he has to make all things new – all this can be summed up in these words, quoted by Jesus: 'What I want is mercy, not sacrifice' (Matthew 9:13; cf. Hosea 6:6).

This truth is the perfect yardstick by which we can tell how genuinely attached to his thought we are.

If I only knew how to contemplate but did not know how to forgive, I should not be one of his.

If I macerated my flesh for his love in all manner of penances but did not know how to open my door to my fellow-man even though my enemy, I should not have understood what his kingdom is.

If I gave up my body to be burned for the triumph of justice but kept a single spot in my heart dominated by a dislike for any one of my fellow-beings, I should be far from Jesus' thought.

And what is the reason for such a radical attitude on the part of Jesus?

Why such a capacity for love, I might even say preference, for the sinner?

The answer, hard as it may be to discern at the outset of one's journey, is simple.

The sinner is the poorest of the poor, the sickest of the sick.

If it is true that God's mercy is attracted by the poor, the sinner will attract it more, being the poorest of the poor.

What is the poverty of the physically naked in comparison with nakedness of spirit?

What is lack of bread, as compared with lack of love?

Who is poorer, Francis, naked but free, or his father, clothed, but idolizing his riches?

There are no limits to the misery of the violent and the cruel, fettered by the senses, worn out by drugs and lust.

There is no greater anguish than of those who, fleeing from life's great challenges, end in the loneliness of an exquisite egotism.

If God is God – and so he is – the hierarchy of happiness begins with him, not from the other end.

The closer we are to God, the happier we are. The further away from him, the poorer.

Sin, which is flight from God, is no fun. It gives no joy, fulfilment or peace, and constantly betrays us.

For those who have tried, for those who know the truth and have tasted the sweetness of God and his house, the sinner is truly unfortunate and calls for their compassion.

For those who have experienced the Absolute, the sinner is someone who will never fulfil himself, always on the run with neither home nor aim.

Where is the sinner's home?

Where is the traitor's joy?

Where is security and stability for anyone who does not believe, hope, love?

This is why the gospel can be summed up in Luke's parable of the Prodigal, the return to the father of the far-away child.

The return is God's victory, God's true joy.

By mercy, God slakes his thirst for love.

Knowing God, even though I know it is possible we may be lost, I am now convinced that all will be saved.

13 'Robbers' Den . . .'

How much I must criticize you, my Church and yet how much I love you!

How you have made me suffer and yet how much I owe you.

I should like to see you destroyed and yet I need your presence.

You have given me so much scandal and yet you have made me understand holiness.

Never in the world have I seen anything more obscurantist, more compromised, more false, yet never have I touched anything more pure, more generous or more beautiful.

How often I have felt like slamming the door of my soul in your face – and how often I have prayed that I might die in your sure arms!

No, I cannot be free of you, for I am one with you, even though not completely you.

Then, too – where should I go?

To build another?

But I cannot build another without the same defects, for they are my own defects I bear within me. And again, if I build one, it will be my Church, and no longer Christ's.

I am old enough to know that I am no better than others.

The other day a friend of mine wrote a letter to a newspaper. 'I am leaving the Church,' he said. 'It is so involved with the rich that it has lost its credibility.'

That hurts me.

Either this person is a sentimentalist, without experience of life, and then I can excuse him – or he is proud, someone who thinks himself better than others, thinks himself more credible than others.

None of us is credible while we are on this earth.

'You think me a saint!' St Francis shouted. 'And do you know, I can still beget children on a prostitute if Christ support me not!'

Credibility is not a human attribute. It is God's alone, and Christ's.

The human attribute is weakness and, every once in a while, the good will to do something good with the help of the grace that spurts from the invisible veins of the visible Church.

Was yesterday's Church any better than today's? Was the Church of Jerusalem any more 'credible' than the Roman?

When Paul arrived in Jerusalem, bearing in his heart his thirst for universality, on the mighty wind of charismatic inspiration, might not the discourses of James on foreskins to be amputated, or the weakness of Peter who was dallying with the rich of those days (the sons and daughters of Abraham) and who gave scandal by dining only with the pure – might not these have given him doubts about the truth of the Church, which Christ had founded fresh as the morning, and made him feel like going off to found another one at Antioch or Tarsus?

Might not St Catherine of Siena, seeing the pope intriguing against her city (and a dirty intrigue it was), the city of her heart, have suddenly decided to take to the Sienese hills, those hills crystalline as the skies, and fashion another Church more crystalline than the Roman, so opaque and obtuse, so sinful, so political?

No, I think not. Both Paul and Catherine knew how to distinguish between the people who composed the Church – the Church's 'personnel', as Maritain called them – and that human society called 'Church', which, unlike all other human societies, 'has received from God a personality that is supernatural, holy, immaculate, pure, indefectible, infallible, beloved of Christ as his spouse, and worthy to be loved by myself as my most sweet mother.'

Here is the mystery of the Church of Christ, the true, impenetrable mystery.

The Church has the power to give me holiness, and it is composed entirely of sinners, each and every member of it. Some sinners!

It has the all-powerful, invincible faith to celebrate the eucharistic mystery ever and again, and it is composed of weak men and women groping in the dark and daily grappling with the temptation to lose faith.

It bears a message of purest ray serene and is incarnate in a dough as dirty as the world is dirty.

It speaks of the Master's sweetness and non-violence, yet has sent armies to disembowel infidels and torture heretics.

It transmits a message of evangelical poverty, and does nothing but collect money and strike alliances with the mighty.

One has only to read the proceedings in the trial of St Joan of Arc at the hands of the Inquisition to be assured that Stalin was not the first to falsify documents and to prostitute judges.

One has only to think of what was done to innocent Galileo to make him sign under duress, to be assured that, however much they may be Church, the people of the Church, the Church's personnel, are evil people, the cheapest personnel that can be had, capable of committing errors as vast as the earth's orbit round the sun.

In vain do we look for anything else from the Church, other than this mystery of infallibility and fallibility, of sanctity and sin, of weakness and courage, of credibility and non-credibility.

Those who dream of anything else but this, are only wasting their time and always having to start again. Furthermore, they demonstrate their failure to understand human beings.

For this is the way human beings are – just as the Church shows them to be – in their wickedness, yet in that invincible courage which faith in Christ has bestowed on them and with which the charity of Christ fortifies their lives.

When I was young, I did not understand why, in spite of Peter's denial, Jesus still wanted him to be the head of the Church, his successor, the first pope. Now I am no longer surprised. I have gradually come to understand that the founding of the Church on the tomb of a traitor, a person terrified by a servant-girl's chatter, is a permanent warning for each of us to stay humble and aware of our own frailty.

No, I shall not leave this Church, founded on so frail a rock, because I should be founding another one on an even frailer rock: myself.

And then, what do rocks matter? What matters is Christ's promise, what matters is the cement that binds the rocks into one: the Holy Spirit. The Holy Spirit alone can build the Church with stones as ill-hewn as we!

The Holy Spirit alone can hold us together, keep us one in spite of ourselves, in spite of the centrifugal force with which our boundless pride endows us.

For myself, when I hear the Church being criticized, I am pleased. I listen as I would to a serious, reflective sermon inspired by a thirst for the good, and a clear, untrammelled vision of things.

'We ought to be poor . . . evangelical . . . we ought not to rely on alliances with the powerful', and so forth and so on.

But in the end, I feel this criticism, levelled against the person of my parish priest, my bishop or my pope, is actually addressed to me. I feel that I am in the same boat, in the same barque of Peter – blood relative that I am to certified sinners and a sinner myself.

And then I try to criticize myself, and perceive how difficult conversion is.

For it could and does happen, that, as I sit in my living-room after a good meal, discussing the burning question of colonialism, I forget all about my wife or my mother in the kitchen washing up. So can you doubt that the spirit of colonialism is deeply entrenched in our hearts?

For it can and does happen, that at the very instant I am furiously excoriating the sin of racial pride committed by whites against blacks, I have to be the fellow who is always right, who tells his father he 'doesn't know anything' being a mere country bumpkin, and who burns a pinch of incense everyday before the idol lucky enough to be the 'Director', or the 'Foreman', or the 'Professor', or, in the case of a woman, the 'Body Beautiful'.

And then I recall the words of Jesus: 'Do not judge, and you will not be judged; because the judgements you give are the judgements you will get, and the amount you measure out is the amount you will be given' (Matthew 7:1–2).

No, it is not wicked to criticize the Church when you love it. It is wicked to criticize it from outside, as though you yourself were pure. It is not wicked to criticize the sin and the ugly things we see. It is wicked to saddle others with them, while believing ourselves to be innocent, poor and meek.

This is wicked.

I wrote everything you have just been reading in this chapter, while I was sitting on the dry, fiery dunes of the African desert. Many years have passed since I returned from Africa to Europe. But I still subscribe with the same awareness to all I said then.

I should only like to add a few things I owe to more recent experience, after finding myself back in the tissue of Christendom and the dough of the contemporary world.

My return to so-called civilization was a frightful shock.

I would rather have died in Africa.

But I am a Little Brother, and my spiritual father, Charles de Foucauld, taught me, shouted at me for all he was worth, that Little Brothers are not hermits, that their isolation in the desert must only be temporary: a week, forty days, a year, ten years (as I spent) – but after that one must then return to one's own people.

The thrust towards the Absolute of God must result in a thrust towards one's fellow-man, as it did with Jesus, as with Francis, as with the Church, especially today.

The Church, that human yet mystical reality alive in each of us, must be at once in the desert of prayer and in the desert of the great bustling city.

This is the way things are.

And I was forced to come back.

To take to the streets with my brothers and sisters, like you.

And suffer, like you, this twofold tension, reducing one to tears.

And try, like you, to repair the gaps in the crumbling walls of a world that is ever the same.

What a shock, my return to so-called modern civilization!

I had the feeling, even before leaving Europe, that things had taken a turn for the worse. But I never could have imagined how grave our crisis was to become.

I never could have imagined we should see the day when we should have terrorism, the mafia and graft on the scale we have them today.

Oh yes, it existed before – there has always been terrorism or anarchy, but not at . . . shall we say, university level? – where it is can warp young people's minds as though they have run mad.

The Mafia existed before but it still had some vestige of shame. It operated in disguise, by justifying itself as the bulwark of the poor against the rich, the weak against the strong.

Now it is totally degenerate, serving only money, power and politcal interests.

Yes, graft existed too. When was a little pinch of graft not a component of the individual? But at the level of city hall, and even the national government . . .!

Relentless as a spreading cancer, evil has infiltrated the vital organs of society, annihilating age-old traditions, over-throwing ancient defences.

The media of social communication are culturally equivocal now, no longer able to oppose the trend, indeed are becoming an immense, anonymous, elusive, insecure echo, and uninten-tionally contributing to the acceleration of the process of dissolution.

A child with television is lost to this world.

Fed exclusively on images, he no longer reads, no longer reasons, meanders aimlessly through life and, unaware, becomes a cipher.

Unbridled sex – like wealth within too easy reach of everyone – intoxicates the young.

Drugs as a substitute for values, an escape from anything disagreeable, spread their deadly snare.

Our first reaction must surely be to say: We have reached the end of an era. The empire has fallen. The reign of darkness has begun.

But what have all these considerations to do with the Church?

Friends, there is a connection. I mention all these things because they have a close connection with our considerations on the Church. A very close connection!

This is one of the discoveries I have made in my long experience of life, something important I have found.

I have found, I have discovered, that the Church is not divided from the world. The Church is the world's soul, the world's conscience, the world's heaven. Precisely because Christ became incarnate, I no longer have the right to divide the good from the bad, the innocent from the wicked, Zacchaeus from Peter, the adulteress from the apostles.

All are a single whole called the Church. And Jesus died for the Church, and Jesus and the Church are functions of each other.

The people of God are a people of saints, prophets and priests, and at the same time a people of sinners, adulterers and tax-gatherers.

When I was a boy, I looked on the Church as separate from the world.

Now I see the Church quite differently.

And on careful thought, I have to admit that the reason I see it differently is that I have learned to see myself differently.

This is where the mystery lies.

This hotch-potch of good and bad, greatness and wretchedness, sanctity and sin, this Church-World, is, at bottom: me.

In me, there is everything. In me lives the world, and the Church.

In me, there is capacity for evil and the yearning for holiness; corrupt nature and sanctifying grace.

In me, there is Adam and there is Christ.

And as all these are in me, so all these things are in others. It is the mystery of Church-World.

The deed of the Father has made me a 'house of prayer'; my own devilish deeds have succeeded in turning it into a 'den of thieves'.

Which being the case ... many things will have to be changed.

Which being the case, I, the Church in my visible form, must present a different face to the world.

I must not present myself to sinners as holy, to the unjust as just, to the pure as pure.

I must be careful not to be too hasty in climbing on to my soap box and preaching to others, or so confidently giving them my brilliant instructions.

It is hard to separate Adam's sin within me from the transparency of Jesus' prophecy there.

It is pride to feel safe and secure in this 'house of prayer' and take no account of Christ's reproach, '. . . you have turned it into a robbers' den' (Mark 11:17).

Do not let us hesitate to say this – Christ's fearsome words against the Temple in Jerusalem applied not only to the Temple, then intent on putting him to death, but to every one of us and every one of our parish churches. Every one of us can become a den of thieves, and so can every one of our churches.

By what authority do we think that, because Jesus has come, we are simply no longer capable of sin, or that the Church no longer runs the risk of putting revenue before prayer?

Well, then?

What am I to do?

My feeling is, the first thing I must do is change my attitude.

If it is true that sin and holiness cohabit in me and I cannot separate what the Church is from what the world is, I ought to be more humble in my attitude toward things going on around me. In future, I must not be so ready to judge others as vessels of the world's sin and feel myself to be the ever-innocent because I belong to the Church.

I am not innocent of the world's sin!

If I so readily raise my voice against sinners, I must be just as ready to accuse myself of the infinite number of things for which I myself am responsible.

What strange things happen in our churches!

It is as though the gospel were not read in them, or at any rate not understood in them. And yet of course anyone can see that it is.

To hear the usual parish sermons, even the ones in the cathedrals and even grander places than that, one has the distinct feeling that, when it comes to sinning, it is always other people who do that, and that we as the Church are always innocent.

Christianity's feudal era, now coming to a close, has left us with an ingrained inability to admit our shortcomings before our 'subordinates'.

If we are parents or teachers, we are careful not to tell our sins before our children or pupils.

And while there has been ever more insistence on the need for confession on the part of the faithful, the habit has become ingrained in us – almost unconsciously – of making believe that sin is impossible for authority and power.

This is not the way things are, and I am certain that in this immense, profound renewal that has been under way since the Council, one of the most important things to be reviewed and rethought is our attitude as church people towards the world.

At bottom it concerns the encounter between sin and holiness, the co-existence in our congregation of Jesus with Magdalene, of Peter who has committed an act of betrayal, with John who stands at the foot of the cross by Mary's side.

It concerns the very mission of the Church in its ability to communicate and reconcile, taught by Jesus.

It is no small matter.

For me, it is the centre of Jesus' whole mission.

The embrace he offers us is the one that 'makes all things new' – and first and foremost my existence.

I am not moved when I receive Communion. But when I make an earnest confession, I weep.

It is not easy to confess deep down inside us, but when we do, conversion is under way.

The true revolution of the soul, the genuine ability to change course, can only occur when I confess my sinfulness.

I know I am a sinner. Anyone who tells me that is not telling me anything I did not already know.

But when I become aware of my wickedness, and proclaim my sinfulness before one and all, then something really serious happens.

For Zacchaeus, the most serious moment of his life was his confession, there, in front of everyone.

From that moment everything was new for him.

Everything was out in the open for all to see.

How strange, it seems to me, is the attitude of some people who insist so much on auricular confession, private confession, as if that were the panacea of Christians!

Not that I fail to understand the importance of spiritual direction, or of private confession of my sins.

But private confession was invented by the Church as a help in our weakness and poverty.

For we are incompetent. We have not yet reached our majority, the maturity, the humility to proclaim our sins in the assembly of the faithful, before one and all. And so the Church in its mercy condescends to smooth the way for us, makes it easy for us to summon up the strength to pull the skeleton out of our cupboard, in the silence of the confessional.

But!

But!

Let us see in the gospel how things are when the Spirit of the Lord hovers near.

Would you like to see three earnest confessions?

Here is the first. It is Peter's, as he stands naked before God on the lake shore: 'Leave me, Lord; I am a sinful man' (Luke 5:8). And round him stood the tiny Church, coming into existence.

Another serious confession, another earnest confession, is that of Zacchaeus, right in the middle of a crowd, and not a crowd of friends either: 'Look, sir, I am going to give half my property to the poor, and if I have cheated anybody I will pay him back four times the amount' (Luke 19:8).

But the most beautiful and dramatic confession we have is the one on Calvary, from the lips of someone who was a worse thief than Zacchaeus.

Luke reports it to us in these words: 'We deserve it, after all,' says the thief, turning towards the other thief, hanging there crucified like him. 'We are only paying the price for what we've done, but this man has done nothing wrong.' Then he turns to Jesus, and adds, full of hope, 'Jesus, remember me when you come into your kingdom' (cf. Luke 23:41–2).

And Jesus' full remission of all his sins is the fitting crown of this, the most worthy confession any dying man could make.

It is hard to confess our sins. It is certainly harder than receiving Communion or the Sacrament of the Sick.

But it is important, and it is especially important to make our confession earnestly.

I must tell you, humbly, that I went to confession each week, as was the practice in my time, especially in the religious life.

But I have to add that I did not enter the confessional without having worked out in advance the trick, the words, to deliver my conscience from my sins but in such a way that the confessor would learn as little as possible.

And dare I mention the confessions I made to show what a fine boy I was?

Poor me!

Forgive me for my weakness. Forgive me too, if I dare say to the bishops (who convened for the synod on the Sacrament of Reconciliation): 'Do not place too much emphasis on confessional-boxes. Place more emphasis on the guts to hear confessions and to confess in the liturgical assembly itself.'

A great deal of emphasis. Perhaps even with clear, unmistakable words.

And since we are dealing with something hard here, something very hard, give us a hand, by setting us an example.

Why should the servant confess and not the employer? Why should the pupil confess and not the teacher?

Why the child and not the parent?

Why the parishioner and not the pastor?

Why the last sinner of God's people and not the first?

We shall be told that history and the baroque centuries have taught us in all sorts of ways that authority is sacrosanct, not to be touched. But . . . How wonderful it was for me to hear Pope John beg forgiveness of the Jews for the suffering inflicted on them by Christians! How fine a thing it was to hear Pope Paul state that Galileo's trial had been unjust!

And when Pope John Paul confessed in Spain, in the name of the Church, the sins committed by the Spanish Inquisition!

These are confessions that do good, that free consciences, that help people understand people, that bind us more closely to our churches – and in the end . . . help us discover what we seek: God himself.

That is something I have never understood better than in the moment of reconciliation: who God is.

14 Farewell

The time has come.

There is a passage in the Psalms that says: 'Our life lasts for seventy years, eighty with good health . . .' (Psalm 90:10).

These words apply to me; I do not find them hard to accept.

I may also say that I don't want to go on much longer; even though I know that the gift of life is great, the gift of death is greater.

Do not be surprised at what I say. It may seem strange, but it is not.

I have told you in every way I can think of, that I believe in God and that I have committed my entire existence to this effort of belief.

Now, precisely in believing, I have come to a conclusion which I want to put as the endpiece to this book about my faith.

God has done great deeds. This is beyond doubt, and we are always saying so in our church services: 'His wisdom made the heavens, and the earth . . .' (cf. Psalm 136:5). And this is no small thing.

'He decides the number of the stars and gives each of them a name' (Psalm 147:4).

He made human beings, and wants them as his children.

He made the Kingdom and destined us for it.

Well, among all those good and beautiful things, he has made one most beautiful of all. Death!

When you hear this for the first time, you may make a wry face or at least be very puzzled.

But there is no reason to be. Let me explain.

Go, some sunny day, to a nursing home, the place where children of refined sensibility today stockpile the elderly.

What does this place make you think of?

What do all those twisted limbs, extinguished eyes and obvious sufferings suggest to you?

I know what they suggest to me: one thing –

'O blessed death, come, come, come, do not delay!'

I know. The most devout of you will say that even a single day of this life counts in completing what is lacking in the sufferings of Christ (cf. Colossians 1:24). I know it, and I believe it, and accept everything that God decrees for me, from this time forward.

I know it!

But I am thinking about a different aspect, over which you cannot reproach me.

I have discovered, among all good and beautiful things God has made, that there is one no less beautiful, as I said, but even more beautiful – and that is death.

Why?

Because it enables me to start again. It enables me to see 'new things'.

Never as now have I understood so well what Scripture says: 'Now I am making the whole of creation new' (Revelation 21:5).

Not that I love death because it dissolves my last remaining strength. I love death because it 'makes all things new'.

Whenever I see a slobbering, trembling old man, I make an effort to think of him in the body of a happy baby. Whenever I look at a woman tragically enduring the ugliness and inroads of old age, the fruit of time, I put my imagination to work and think of her as a teenage girl racing through fields of flowers to meet her sweetheart.

I love death because it gives me back life.

I love death because I believe in the resurrection.

Now, that is something I can get excited about!

What would have been the point of all my efforts to believe, of all my hoping against hope if, when I got to that moment, I were to settle for nothingness? Or worse, immobility, an eternal paralysis?

No, I do not settle for that, and I tell you, or rather, I shout at you: 'I believe in the life everlasting!'

I believe in my everlasting body as an immortal babe.

I believe in my running like a little boy to meet my God, as when long ago, after school, I ran like crazy to meet my father, who had come to take me for a walk in the fields along the Po.

But even more I believe in death, because I shall finally see the Kingdom, which here below I have only descried through the mist, and dreamed about.

I shall see the Church in its final transparency.

I shall see my mother again.

I shall see my friends again.

I shall see righteousness.

I shall see the banquet.

I shall see people at peace at last and able to love one another.

I shall see Christ!

There, I know, I shall be thunderstruck at his beauty and shall never have to leave him again.

Also because, as the 'Lamb that was slain', he has become 'worthy to open the scroll and break the seals' (cf. Revelation 5:6, 2).

And he will open them.

And we shall read all the mysteries. We shall know the whys and wherefores of history, of the succession of the generations, of all the tears and bloodshed.

Who turns the pages of the Book will be Mary of Nazareth, the only creature worthy to help her son in explaining these things to us.

Mark well, I am not dreaming; I am reading my faith, my hope.

This is why I tell you that death is one of God's great inventions.

What would we be without death?

Who feels like living on in a nursing home where people have put you with all their love and pills?

Not I.

And I invoke death as a transit.

This will be my Passover.

This will be the gate of heaven.

This will be the resurrection.

And here I must tell you another secret I have discovered recently: I am sure, when death's hammer smashes me like an olive; in that instant I shall see all the whys of life: in that instant I shall say 'Now I understand why death is this great fact throughout the cosmos. In death was hidden the very secret of life.'

And a great 'Oh!' of wonder will rise from my being.

Quake not, then, my soul, and have no fear.

Look straight ahead and smile one last time.

As the Spirit glided over chaos in the beginning and God created the universe, now he will return, to hover once more and make all things new again.

Precisely because I believe in God, I know what death is, and it cannot frighten me.

Or at least it will only frighten me mentally – and with good reason, for I shall feel such a powerful wrench and an even more obvious difference.

Come then, O death, my death!

I shall welcome you as my sweetheart, I shall embrace you as my sister.

I shall greet you as mother.

I do not ask you not to be painful; the memory of my brother Jesus' death will remind me to keep quiet and acquiesce.

I shall ask you to have mercy on my weakness.

I shall ask you to make me one with all my fellow-beings dying in pain.

I shall ask you to help me forget all about my sins and be brave enough to believe in God's mercy.

I shall ask you to act quickly. Yes, this I shall ask of you.

But more than anything else, I shall ask you to give me your love right away.

Here-below, forsaking all the rest, I have been left with three things, and I have sought to live them: 'faith, hope and love' (1 Corinthians 13:13).

As to faith, I have succeeded, a tiny crumb of a bit. I have always been fond of faith as of a great risk to run, and I have loved to stake it all like a master-card in my hand.

As to hope, I have done better. My mother transmitted to me in my blood her unbeatable optimism, her urge to sing and live.

But as to charity, to love, what are we to say?

This is where my weak point has been.

Here I have not succeeded very well. On the contrary, I have barely understood what the rapture of service and total self-giving can be.

Paul's mighty statement, '... if I have faith in all its fullness, to move mountains, but without love, then I am nothing at all' (1 Corinthians 13:2), has always tormented me and made me weep, too.

In my boundless inability to love, God has revealed to me what God's folly is.

Yes, through the darkness of my selfishness, he has shown me the blinding lights of his love.

What a clash, between the poverty of human love and the madness of God!

How I have suffered in the darkness of my rational way of judging things!

And how clear within me was the vision of the 'emergency exit' that would have saved me: the madness of love!

But I was unable to open it, being held back by the fear of losing all. I actually had the idea that, were I to give myself ... I would lose everything!

On the contrary, I should have gained everything!

As you did, Jesus, on Calvary.

Nor have I been able to ask, with St Francis:

Lord Jesus, two graces I ask of you before I die.

First, in my soul and in my body, to feel as far as possible, the sorrow which you, sweet Jesus, endured in the hour of your most bitter passion.

Second, in my heart, as far as possible, to feel that extraordinary love with which you, O Son of God, were inflamed, to the point of being willing to undergo so great a passion for us sinners.

No, my God, I have not been able.

And this is why I want to die.

So that I can go instantly mad under the hammer blows of your Spirit.

So I can vault the barricade of my own insuperable limitations.

What I have been incapable of doing here, I count on doing at my Passover, when you will at last come into my being and burn it away as in the fire.

What joy, Lord, this, your loving-madness! When I think that you will transmit this madness to me too, I descry the reality of the Kingdom, as a transit from the human to the divine, for which you are preparing us – and as the joy of living for ever with you.

What more shall I say to you in my leave-taking, old friends?

I do not know.

Shall I say that you will go through hard times? No need to tell you that; everyone knows it.

The very stones cry out. But there are two things to be specially on guard against, since they are able to increase the amount of trouble and sorrow already prevalent in the world. Both are things opposed to life and extremely dangerous: the man who does not work – who no longer commits himself – and the woman who doesn't want to have children.

For me these are signs of a particularly frightening tomorrow.

When a young man no longer feels the need to build, to make, to do, to 'get involved', it is as though his life-force, the spring of his existence, were waning.

It is even worse when a young woman no longer dreams about having a baby, indeed arranges things so as not to have one. She will have to go through very bitter moments when she looks back on this.

I would advise you strongly against these temptations. Be brave and resist them. They are characteristic of the modern world, a world going rotten at its pagan roots.

Do not go into life without dreaming of building yourselves

a house to live in, a vocation to find fulfilment in, and children to play with.

I know that you have temptations against faith. How could it be otherwise, in a world where man, by force of intellect, has succeeded in walking on the moon and in transforming the earth into a single insufferable gangster-land by his sick heart?

When you are tempted, do not retreat a single step. God will help you.

And perhaps the better to help you, he will give you a little poverty – but the real kind, not the romantic kind flaunted by European Christians of my time.

He may even be forced to lead you back to the Egypt of ancient slavery, or even to the dreadful loneliness of Babylon.

Whatever happens to you, do not retreat a single step.

This too will pass, and God abides for ever.

For me, all this is over and I have the feeling of having attained the goal.

But if I have won, it's because God has won, and if you too win it will be because God wins in you.

Together let us recall Jesus' words when he bade farewell to his own:

'Do not let your hearts be troubled. Trust in God . . .' (John 14:1).

Ah, look . . . we could finish by reading one of the last pages of the Book of Revelation together:

I saw a new heaven and a new earth; the first heaven and the first earth had disappeared now, and there was no longer any sea.

I saw the holy city, and the new Jerusalem, coming down from God out of heaven, as beautiful as a bride all dressed for her husband.

Then I heard a loud voice call from the throne, '. . . Here God lives among men. He will make his home among them; they shall be his people, and he will be their God; his name is God-with-them. He will wipe away all tears from their eyes; there will be no more death, and no more mourning or sadness. The world of the past has gone' (Revelation 21:1–4).

And the answer is contained in the splendid finale:
'Yes, I am coming soon!' Amen!
'Come, Lord Jesus!
'May the grace of the Lord Jesus be with you all. Amen!' (cf. Revelation 22:20–1).